Essential Seamanship

Essential Seamanship

BY

RICHARD HENDERSON

Cornell Maritime Press

Centreville, Maryland

Library of Congress Cataloging-in-Publication Data

Henderson, Richard.
        Essential seamanship / by Richard Henderson.—1st ed.
          p. cm.
        Includes index.
        ISBN 0-87033-456-5 (pbk.) : $8.95
        1. Seamanship. 2. Boats and boating. I. Title.
GV777.5.H46 1994
797.1—dc20   94-10132

Manufactured in the United States of America

First edition

To my sister,
Weenie Leader,
with fond memories of the
early days aboard *Kelpie*

Contents

Introduction

Seamanship is a very broad term applicable to a great many aspects of managing a vessel. It is defined in *The Dictionary of Sailing*, by Joachim Schult, as the "general term of covering all the skills and arts which, combined with experience and the ability to improvise, enable a sailor to face every situation at sea, i.e. boat handling, repairs and maintenance, navigation, weather lore, knowledge of the right of way rules, etc."

The purpose of this book is to present in condensed form the most important and practical elements of seamanship and nautical knowledge needed by today's small boat skipper. It is also intended as a ready, up-to-date, onboard reference. Yarns and lengthy discussions are limited in order to broaden the coverage and provide essential details within a book of handy size. I'm assuming that this book will be read by at least some novices, so most nautical terms are defined when they are introduced.

Regarding the author's qualifications to write on this subject, I can only say that for more than six decades I've been learning seamanship by trial and error. The latter still occurs on more than a few occasions; so I give the reader fair warning: if you see me on the water, don't necessarily do as I do, but do as I write.

Another admonition is, don't think you can learn from books alone. They can be extremely helpful, but real proficiency can be attained only with practice. There are few activities more rewarding than developing skills in seamanship through building knowledge, learning theories, and then putting the information into practice.

Essential Seamanship

1. Boat Evaluation and Fitting Out

*You could sense her lines, their round practicality,
and get pleasure . . . in knowing, somehow, despite
lack of experience, that they were 'just right.'*
                                            —*Charles Landry*

An important element of seamanship is the ability to study a vessel and recognize her suitability in design, construction, and preparation for exposure to adverse conditions in unprotected waters. Whether skippering, crewing, or considering a boat for purchase, a competent sailor should recognize the purpose for which the boat was designed, be able to predict her behavior with reasonable accuracy, and know if she is properly equipped. Purpose relates to how the boat will be used; for example, whether she will be used for daysailing or fishing in sheltered waters or passagemaking offshore. It should be kept firmly in mind, however, that even if a boat never leaves protected waters, there may be times when she is caught by a sudden squall or exposed to abnormally rough conditions. Where seaworthiness is concerned, there should always be a healthy margin of safety.

HOW DESIGN AFFECTS BEHAVIOR

To predict a boat's behavior, one should consider her lines or hull shape, appendages, rig, underwater configuration, and a few design ratios. The following list of generalities

3

includes good rules of thumb for appraising a vessel's performance and seaworthiness:

— Flare at the bow is helpful in deflecting spray and providing reserved buoyancy in head seas.

— Sheer is helpful in keeping the bow from burying and providing stern elevation above following seas.

— Freeboard should be moderate, as too little of it allows a sailboat to bury her rail and a powerboat to ship water, while excessive freeboard causes undesirable windage and raises the center of gravity, adversely affecting stability.

— Overhangs provide reserve buoyancy and reduce wetted surface for a sailboat in light airs, but excessive overhangs, perhaps greater than one third of the waterline length, may cause pounding in a seaway and reduce speed in moderate winds due to shortness of length at the waterline.

— A displacement (non-planing) hull's speed is based on its waterline length. Top speed in knots (nautical miles per hour) of such a hull is about 1.34 times the square root of its waterline length. The longer the waterline the greater the speed potential.

— Planing occurs when a boat skims over the top of the water rather than plowing through it. When on a full plane, a boat's speed will be about two or more times the square root of the waterline length. Semi-planing begins at a speed of about 1.6 times the square root of the waterline length. Exactly when a boat will plane depends on such factors as hull shape, displacement, and seas.

— An asymmetrical hull, one with a fine bow and full stern, is generally effective in head seas or resistant to extreme pitching, and has high initial stability or power to carry sail. The drawback of such a form is that the hull lacks balance and tends to cause erratic steering at slow

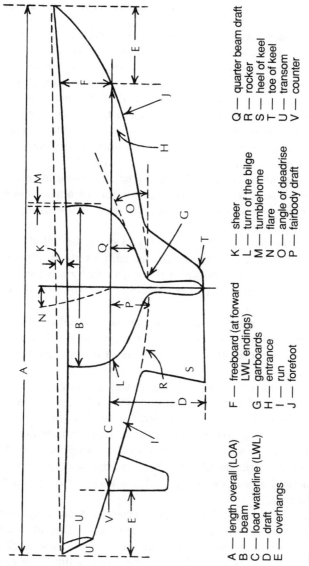

A — length overall (LOA)
B — beam
C — load waterline (LWL)
D — draft
E — overhangs

F — freeboard (at forward LWL endings)
G — garboards
H — entrance
I — run
J — forefoot

K — sheer
L — turn of the bilge
M — tumblehome
N — flare
O — angle of deadrise
P — fairbody draft

Q — quarter beam draft
R — rocker
S — heel of keel
T — toe of keel
U — transom
V — counter

Fig. 1-1. Hull nomenclature

speeds in powerboats and perhaps an overly strong weather helm (see chapter 2) when sailboats are heeled.

— A symmetrical hull, one with a fuller bow and finer stern, is usually easier to steer but more tender (heels more easily) and may pitch more actively in head seas.

— Weight in a boat's ends will normally adversely affect her performance in head seas. Concentrating weight amidships tends to prevent the bow from burying and allows it to lift more easily without wasting energy.

— Beam increases initial stability or stiffness and power to carry sail, but extreme beam detracts from ultimate stability and causes additional resistance to headway in rough waters.

— Centerboard boats need plenty of beam for initial stability but they are subject to capsizing in strong winds. Keel/centerboard boats may risk capsizing by wave action in the most severe weather offshore, especially when seas are on the beam.

— As a very general rule, most normal sailboats carrying ballast in or on their keels need at least one third of their displacement allotted to ballast weight for adequate stability.

— A significant factor relating to seaworthiness is boat size. Due to the effect of scaling laws, the larger boat generally fares better in heavy weather than a smaller one with respect to roll inertia, initial stability, and wind velocity. Comparing geometrically similar sister boats of different sizes, the smaller one feels a stronger wind of given velocity, heels more easily, and has less inertia to resist rollovers.

— Extremely light displacement provides good buoyancy and speed downwind but may cause pounding in head seas, lacks ultimate stability, and may mean less strength or puncture resistance (unless the construction is of exceptional quality). On the other hand, extremely heavy displacement sacrifices speed and buoyancy for strength and resistance to capsizing. Moderate displacement seems the best compromise for cruising.

—An offshore monohull sailboat needs a healthy stability range. She should at least be able to recover from a 120-degree rolldown. A stability range of 130 to 140 degrees or higher is preferable.

—When the stability range of a normal monohull sailboat is not known, a commonly used method of determining adequate ultimate stability is with the simple capsize screening formula: maximum beam in feet is divided by the cube root of displacement in cubic feet. (Displacement in cubic feet is obtained by dividing the boat's weight in pounds by 64). The result of this calculation should be no greater than 2.

—Flat or shallow V-bottomed hulls tend to pound more than round-bottomed hulls, but the latter tend to roll more in beam seas, especially in powerboats without the steadying effect of sails.

—Planing powerboats with deep V-bottoms having an almost constant angle of deadrise carried aft (with a fairly deep V-bottom at the stern) generally pound the least in head seas, but such a hull is more difficult to push onto a plane.

—Chines (sharp corners where the bottom meets the topsides on V-bottom boats) are normally low at the bows of cruising powerboats, but they should be reasonably high to lessen pounding and head resistance at low speeds.

—Warped V-hulls with deep V forward and shallow V aft, often with rounded chines (similar to Maine lobster boats), have proven a good compromise between speed and seaworthiness for small- to medium-size powerboats in choppy seas.

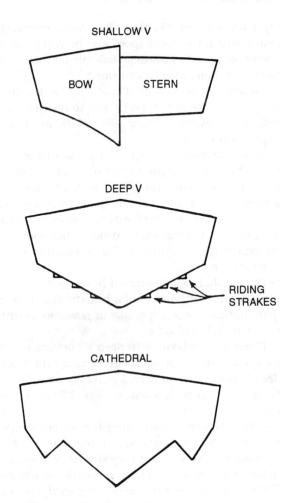

Fig. 1-2. V-bottom hull configurations

— Cathedral hulls (centrally V'd but with smaller V'd sponsons on each side) and other tunnel types of power-boat hulls often minimize pounding in moderate seas partly because of the cushioning effect of air in the longitudinal tunnels.

— Many high-powered motorboats, especially those with deep V-bottoms aft need trim tabs controllable at the helm to assist in planing and hold the bow down at high speeds.

— Many round-bottom cruising powerboats need roll control devices such as bilge keels, antiroll tanks, fin stabilizers, flopper stoppers (fisherman's paravanes suspended from booms) or steadying sails.

— Keels or skegs forward of propellers afford good protection against damaging propellers or shafts from groundings or collisions with flotsam.

— A long keel produces greater directional stability but slower helm response than a longitudinally short fin keel.

— A short keel reduces wetted surface for greater sailing speed in light airs and creates good helm response, but at some cost in helm steadiness and in relatively deep draft for the prevention of excessive leeway at low speeds.

— A boat with short keel should have her rudder detached from her keel and moved as far as possible aft for the most effective steering control. Her rudder can either be an outboard type (hung on the transom), a spade (attached only to a rudder stock that penetrates the hull), or a skeg-mounted rudder.

— Outboard rudders are practical on boats with very little overhang aft, but they are subject to ventilation (aeration of the submerged blade) and therefore must be deep. Spade rudders can provide very quick and easy response but will stall more easily, can rarely if ever be left unattended, and may lack the inherent strength of a skeg-mounted rudder.

— Underwater appendages, with the possible exception of those on strictly racing sailboats, should be raked aft sufficiently to discourage snagging seaweed, kelp, nets, lines, etc.

— The Bruce number provides a simple method of evaluating a sailboat's performance. It is obtained by dividing the square root of the sail area (in square feet) by the cube root of displacement (in pounds). When the Bruce number is under 1.1, a monohull is apt to be sluggish in light airs.

— Another simple formula for estimating light air performance is the sail area to wetted surface ratio (sail area in square feet divided by wetted surface area in square feet). The result should be well over 2 for lively performance in light winds. Wetted surface area for most stock designs can be obtained from IMS (International Measurement System) rating certificates of sister boats.

CONSTRUCTION AND SAFETY FEATURES

A competent seaman need not have the knowledge of a yacht surveyor, but should develop an ever watchful eye, the "seaman's eye," for any kind of failure in the vessel and her gear. He or she should also have some idea about how well the boat is built and how the boat might react in the worst possible weather and sea conditions. Here are some safety and construction features, some of which need periodic checking.

— Every easily capsizable boat needs sufficient flotation to prevent her from sinking. An open cockpit centerboarder should have enough flotation to keep her floating level in a swamped condition with the top of her centerboard trunk far above water. Check the condition of foam flotation and flotation compartments.

—Multihulls have relatively short ranges of transverse stability and are very difficult to right when upside down, but most are unballasted and so will serve as crude life rafts after they have turned turtle. Even if built of buoyant material, however, they need sufficient flotation to counteract heavy weights onboard such as ground tackle and engines. For coastal multihulls sailing in relatively smooth water, it is often desirable to have flotation at the masthead to prevent inverting and facilitate righting.

—An open cockpit daysailer needs a high degree of self righting ability. This means that the boat should be able to recover from a severe knockdown, and in the event of a capsize, be easily righted by crew standing on the centerboard. Self righting ability is obtained or enhanced by the placement of ample flotation, normally below the gunwales.

—Any boat used in exposed waters should have a self-bailing cockpit—a watertight well with large scuppers that will quickly drain the cockpit should it be filled by a sea breaking aboard. The cockpit sole of a self-bailing cockpit should be at least .02 times the waterline length above the load waterline. Cockpit drain time should be three minutes or less.

—Companionway sills should be high above the cockpit sole, preferably above the main deck level, to prevent downflooding in the event the cockpit is filled. Offshore boats without this feature need a drop board that can be locked in place.

—Vee'd companionways (with the top of the vertical opening wider than the bottom) especially need lock-in drop boards as the boards will fall out if they are only slightly lifted.

—There should be no uncovered openings in the sides of cockpit wells, and cockpit seat lockers should be capable of being securely dogged.

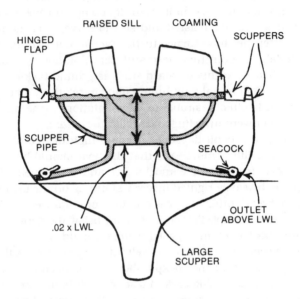

Fig. 1-3. A flooded cockpit well

—Hatches on offshore sailboats should be on or close to the vessel's centerline. All hatches need gaskets and dogs.
—Windows on offshore boats should be as small as possible, well supported, and held in place by sturdy frames. Boats with large windows need storm shutters (rigid coverings). Polycarbonates such as Lexan or Tuffak offer high strength for glazing and shuttering.
—Ventilators on offshore boats need a means of closing (with screw plates or perhaps bags). Dorade vents (water trap types) should have their cowls abaft the standpipes penetrating the deck, and the vents should be as close as possible to the boat's centerline (see illustration).

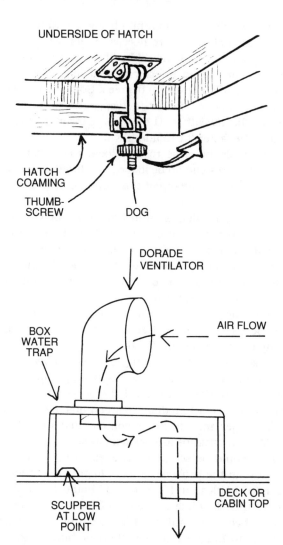

UNDERSIDE OF HATCH

HATCH
COAMING

THUMB-
SCREW

DOG

DORADE
VENTILATOR

AIR FLOW

BOX
WATER
TRAP

DECK OR
CABIN TOP

SCUPPER
AT LOW
POINT

Fig. 1-4. Top, *hatch dog;* bottom, *Dorade ventilator*

— The fewer holes through a hull below the waterline the better. Those holes that are necessary (for scuppers, engine water intake, etc.) should be fitted with valves. Gate valves are considered inferior to seacocks that can be closed by turning a lever 90 degrees. Some boats need a valve for the engine exhaust to keep water from entering in the roughest weather. The deeper a through-hull hole is located the faster it can admit water.

— Sinks should be close to a sailboat's centerline, and plumbing fixtures should be looped and fitted with siphon breakers (vents at the top of the loops) to prevent back-siphoning.

— Flow-through toilets should have their bowls higher than the waterline to prevent flooding in the event of check valve failure or failure to close seacocks.

— All hoses leading to seacocks should be attached with double hose clamps but only when there is sufficient length of pipe to accept two.

— Offshore boats should have an extra engine starter switch below or in a shelter as a precaution against shorting out from cockpit flooding.

— There should be adequate bilge pumps. On boats larger than daysailers there should be one fixed pump on deck, operable from the helm, and one belowdecks operable from the cabin. Double-action diaphragm pumps that can move 30 gallons per minute are recommended for offshore boats. Manual backups are needed for electric pumps.

— Tanks should be securely fastened to the hull, especially those in the bow where there is greater motion. All tanks need baffles, and fuel tanks should be grounded and have their fuel line at the top of the tank. Metal fuel lines attached to the hull need flexible tubing at sections vulnerable to fatigue from vibration or hull flexing. Air vents on fuel tanks should lead to the boat's exterior and be looped or bent into a circle to keep out water.

—All boats need grounding for lightning protection to provide a low resistance path from the lightning strike to ground and also to help bleed off the buildup of static electricity. A metal mast (or sail track on a wood mast) should be grounded to external keel ballast or a ground plate. In addition, masthead shrouds and stays should be grounded. They are sometimes grounded to seacocks, but this risks destruction of the seacocks and possible flooding. Minimal protection can be had by clamping to an upper shroud a heavy copper cable supporting a ground plate held at least 2 feet below the water surface. For best protection there should be a pointed copper rod at least 6 inches high or air terminal, such as the Lightning Master, fastened to the top of the mast.

—Bolted-on fin keels need ample support in the form of floor timbers or web frames spread over a large area. Nuts for keel bolts (and any fittings or chain-plates) need periodic inspection to see that they are tight.

—Every keel boat needs a deep sump for the collection of bilge water. It should be deep enough to allow efficient pumping and to keep water from rolling up into lockers and bunks when the boat heels.

—There should be plenty of bolted-on grab rails above and belowdecks.

—There should be no sharp corners below or elsewhere against which a crew member could lurch or fall.

—Decks and steps that are not raw teak should be skid-proofed with rough but nonabrasive material to prevent the crew from slipping.

—All bolted fittings should have large backing plates or else be bolted to areas that are heavily reinforced.

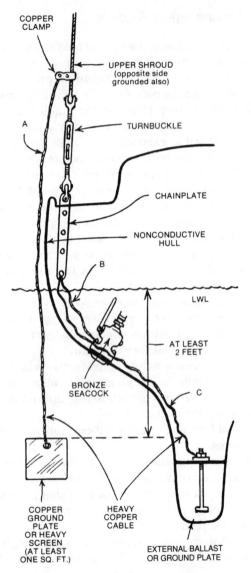

Fig. 1-5. Lightning protection: A, minimal protection; B, risky practice; C, safest practice.

— All shelves should have adequate fiddles (rails) to keep contents in place when heeled or rolled in rough weather. The accompanying illustration shows a removable fiddle for a fore and aft bookshelf. (Shock chord illustrated holds the books in place no matter how many are removed).

— Drawers need locking notches (as illustrated), but in addition, offshore boats need removable safety drop pins to prevent open drawers from sliding all the way out in heavy weather.

— All lockers need mechanical latches (not magnetic fasteners) on locker doors, normally in the forms of sliding bar bolts or internal latches that can be reached through *large* finger holes. Even icebox lids on offshore boats need latches.

— A forward hatch is important not only for ventilation and convenience in stowing sails, but also for an alternate escape exit.

— All sailboats, with the possible exception of small daysailers, should have pulpits and lifelines at least 24 inches high. It is best to have lower as well as upper lifelines, and they should be periodically inspected for security.

— Keep a watchful eye for leaks. Wooden boats and those made of fiberglass with plywood or balsa core are particularly vulnerable to damage from leaks. Look for stains and check the decks for mushiness. Your nose is also a valuable tool for detecting rot or mildew that could lead to rot.

— To prevent rot, stop leaks by caulking, rebedding, and/or replacing or tightening fastenings. Also see that all lockers and tightly sealed spaces belowdecks are ventilated.

— An important area that needs occasional inspection on a fiberglass boat is the hull-deck joint. For rugged offshore duty the hull and deck should be bolted together and preferably bonded with a semiflexible bedding.

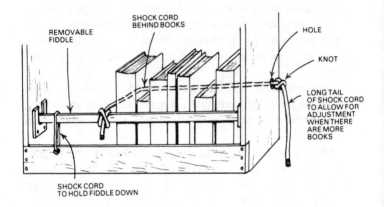

REMOVABLE FIDDLE

SHOCK CORD BEHIND BOOKS

HOLE

KNOT

LONG TAIL OF SHOCK CORD TO ALLOW FOR ADJUSTMENT WHEN THERE ARE MORE BOOKS

SHOCK CORD TO HOLD FIDDLE DOWN

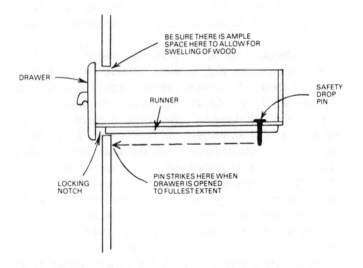

BE SURE THERE IS AMPLE SPACE HERE TO ALLOW FOR SWELLING OF WOOD

DRAWER

RUNNER

SAFETY DROP PIN

LOCKING NOTCH

PIN STRIKES HERE WHEN DRAWER IS OPENED TO FULLEST EXTENT

Fig. 1-6. Top, *fore and aft bookshelf fiddle*; bottom, *safetied drawer*

—See that there is access to every part of the bilge, electric wiring, fastenings that secure all fittings, the stuffing box, valves, and all parts of the engine.

—The entrance (bow just under and above the waterline) is one of the most vulnerable areas on an offshore boat. This area should be reinforced with stringers and/or a semibulkhead to withstand the force of head seas.

—There should be no hardspots—areas of the hull made rigid by internal structural supports surrounded by flexible areas—a condition that could possibly result in fatigue cracking at the points of abrupt change from flexibility to inflexibility. Rigid transverse members should not be allowed to press directly against the hull but against longitudinal stiffeners that gradually distribute the pressure over a wide area. Hardspots often can be detected by looking at reflections on the topsides.

—Fiberglass reinforcements should be made with overlapping layers of cloth so that there is gradual thickening. Abrupt discontinuities of thickness can cause hardspots that are subject to fatigue stress.

—Cabin tops on offshore boats should be well crowned (curved) to resist inverting (oil-canning) and supported internally with beams or bulkheads, and posts and/or dodger coamings.

—Windows and doorways in areas of stress should be oval shaped or at least have rounded corners to prevent stress cracking which usually starts at sharp corners.

—Mast steps need occasional inspection to see that they are not being corroded or crushed by the tremendous downward thrust of the mast. A deck-stepped mast needs a sturdy post (or metal channel beam straddling posts) directly under the mast.

—Bulkheads in way of the mast often are subjected to severe strain, especially when chain-plates are fastened

Fig. 1-7. A rounded doorway, handhold, rounded corners, and support pipes on a Navy 44 (Photo by William E. Brooks, III)

to them. Occasionally inspect the tabbing (fiberglass tape joining a bulkhead to the hull) and the areas around chain-plates.

— Before any offshore passage carefully inspect the skeg and rudder for strength and security. Be wary of spade rudders with stocks and internal arms made of aluminum.

— Sacrificial zincs are needed for the alleviation of galvanic or stray current corrosion, especially on metal boats or any boats where dissimilar metals are used underwater. Zincs need periodic inspections and replacement. The faster a zinc deteriorates the greater the degree of corrosion.

EQUIPMENT

Every boater should know not only what equipment is required by law but also what additional gear is needed on a well-equipped boat. Of course, the amount of gear carried will depend on the size of the boat and where she is going. Bear in mind, however, that required equipment is minimal and is seldom if ever all that is needed. Legal requirements by U.S. Coast Guard standards depend on the classification of boats according to size: Class A is 16 feet or less in length; Class 1, 16 to 26 feet; Class 2, 26 to 40 feet; and Class 3, 40 to 65 feet.

Minimum Required Equipment

PFD—One PFD (personal flotation device) for each person on board. In U.S. waters PFDs must be approved by the Coast Guard. They are classified according to type: Type I PFD is an offshore life jacket or bib designed to turn and float an unconscious person with his or her face out of water. Type II, a close-to-shore buoyancy aid (usually a vest or yoke design) can also protect an unconscious victim, but it lacks the buoyancy of a Type I. Type III is merely a flotation aid, usually in the form of a small vest, and it affords less protection for an unconscious victim. Type IV is a throwable type such as a buoyant cushion, ring, or horseshoe buoy. Boats under 16 feet need one Type I, II, III, or IV PFD per person, while boats from 16 to 65 feet need one Type I, II, or III per person and also at least one Type IV.

Sound makers—A whistle (horn) and bell (for anchoring in fog) for boats 12 meters (39.4 feet) or longer (see chapter 5). Smaller boats shall be provided with "some other means of making an efficient sound signal."

Flame arrestor—One approved backfire flame arrestor on each carburetor of all inboard engines installed after 4/25/40.

Ventilation—Engine ventilation with at least two ducts with cowls to ventilate efficiently the bilges of boats built after 4/25/40 using gasoline or other fuel having a flash-point less than 110°F. Except on open boats, all gasoline powered motorboats built after 7/31/80 are required to have ventilation blowers.

Distress signals—Visual distress signals are required on all boats operating at night and, with a few exceptions, such as Class A and manually propelled boats, during the day. These signals include distress flares, hand or floating orange smoke signals, parachute and meteor flares, electric distress light (that signals SOS), and an orange flag (with black square and solid circle). The simplest combination to meet legal requirements is three hand-held red flares for day or night use. Coast Guard approved pyrotechnic devices can be no more than forty-two months old.

Fig. 1-8. *Safety gear, including a PFD, a dry chemical fire extinguisher, flares, safety belt, signal light, throw rope, and damage control plugs*

Fire extinguishers—Portable fire extinguishers are required unless there are fixed extinguishing systems in Class A and Class 1 boats. Required Coast Guard approved extinguishers are marked with letters (A for combustible materials fires, B for flammable liquid fires, and C for electrical fires) and Roman numerals indicating size (I is the smallest size and II the next larger size). A Class A or 1 boat with no fixed system needs at least one B-I portable extinguisher unless she is an outboard boat built in a way that vapors cannot be trapped. A Class 2 boat needs at least two B-I extinguishers when there is no fixed extinguishing system but only one B-I if there is a fixed system. A Class 3 boat needs at least three B-I extinguishers or a B-I and a B-II when there is no fixed system. If there is a fixed system, two B-Is are required or one B-II. Contents of approved B extinguishers include foam (effective on A as well as B fires), dry chemical (effective on C as well as B fires), and CO_2 (carbon dioxide—can be used on A, B, or C but should be followed by water on A).

Lights—Navigation lights are required under the rules of the road (see Chapter 5).

Minimum Additional Gear

The following equipment is needed but not required by law:

Personal gear—The competent seaman should always carry a knife, preferably one with a marlinespike, screwdriver, and shackle opener. Also needed are boat shoes (with nonskid soles), a tight fitting hat for sun protection, dark glasses, and proper foul weather gear.

Bailers—A small, open boat needs a bailing scoop or can, large sponge, and often a sturdy bucket. A bailing scoop can be made out of a plastic jug (perhaps a Clorox bottle with handle) by cutting off the container's bottom at an angle and tightly screwing on its top. Larger craft need a portable pump with long hose even if there is a fixed bilge pump or two.

Ground tackle—Every boat needs at least one anchor suitable for the local seabed and an anchor line of sufficient scope (length) to provide at least a 7 to 1 scope to depth ratio (see Chapter 9). Large cruisers should have a minimum of three anchors (details in Chapter 9).

MOB (Man overboard) devices—Every boat, even one under 16 feet that is equipped with type I, II, or III PFDs should carry several buoyant cushions that are readily available and can be thrown to a person who has fallen overboard. Lifeslings (see Chapter 7) are recommended on shorthanded medium- to large-size boats. An offshore passagemaker needs a heaving line of floating rope and a man-overboard pole attached to buoy with small sea anchor and floating strobe light (see Chapter 7).

Auxiliary power—Engineless craft should carry a paddle or rowing/sculling oars or a tender that can tow the mother vessel. Single-screw powerboats may want a small jury sail, auxiliary outboard motor, or at least a radio to call for help in the event of engine failure.

Extra Fuel—Small powerboats need spare approved containers of fuel. Standard advice is the ⅓ rule: allow ⅓ of fuel for the passage to destination, ⅓ for the return passage, and ⅓ for reserve.

Navigation equipment—Any vessel above the size of a rowboat used very close to shore needs a compass and at least one local chart. A binocular is highly recommended. Basic instruments include dividers and parallel rules. A depth sounder or at least a lead line is important, especially on boats of deep draft (see Chapter 6).

Lights—Aside from required navigation lights, there should be a waterproof flashlight or two aboard any boat if there is any possibility of being out after dark. It is a good idea to carry a portable anchor light even if there is a masthead light. Offshore boats should carry a spare kerosene lamp or two and portable battery-powered navigation lights in the event of electric power failure. High-intensity strobe flashers are effective for emergencies. Small pocket strobes can be carried by the on-deck crew at night.

Basic tools—For a small boat these include pliers, a screwdriver or two, and a knife. Larger boats need more tools such as wrenches (including an adjustable end wrench large enough to fit the largest nut on the boat), hammer or hatchet, files, needle-nose pliers, hacksaw with extra blades, vise-grip pliers, etc. Offshore passagemakers additionally need such items as a drill, wrecking bar, plane and/or Surform, chisel, clamps, monkey wrenches, etc. Of course, boats with engines should have all tools necessary for engine servicing and emergency repairs. Don't forget squirt cans of lubricating and penetrating oil and also anticorrosion sprays.

Spares—Sailboats especially should carry many spares of small gear. More common items are blocks, shackles, hanks, and cotter pins. There should be plenty of spare lines in assorted lengths and sizes and extra sail stops. Electrical spares include small batteries, bulbs, and fuses. Motorcraft, especially those that cruise long distances, should have some spare engine parts such as filters, belts, distributor caps, points, water pump impeller, spark plugs, coil, and of course, extra lubricating oil.

First aid kit—Essential first aid supplies for a daysailer or small motorboat operating close to shore are: bandages (including ample Band-Aids), sun block (with a sun protection factor (SPF) of at least 15), lip ointment (for sun protection), tweezers, adhesive tape, seasickness medicine (I like Bucladin), aspirin or equivalent, and a first aid book. Larger boats, especially those venturing offshore, need many more items, such as medicine for digestive (gastrointestinal) problems, antibiotics for infections, pain-killers, burn ointments, large rolls of gauze, etc. It would make sense to consult a doctor for complete medical supplies before making a long offshore passage.

Sewing kit—This is needed to whip the ends of lines that are unravelling, for lashings, and to repair sails. The kit should contain sail needles, thread, a palm (for pushing the needle), beeswax (to preserve the thread), balls of twine including marline (heavy waxed twine), a fid or mar-linespike, and special tools for splicing braided line (see Chapter 2).

Damage control kit—The farther a vessel ventures away from shore, the more complete her damage control kit should be. It should contain at least several rolls of repair tape (sail, electrical, and duct tape), tubes of sealant (polysulfide or polyurethane and silicone rubber); caulking cotton; and tapered, wooden, damage control plugs that can be inserted into round holes (plugs are often secured to seacocks in case of their failure). A collision mat (a watertight cloth with lashing lines attached) is desirable on an offshore boat.

Fenders and docking lines—Even boats that are moored on permanent anchors will occasionally land at docks or raft-up with other vessels, so ample fenders and dock lines should be readily available on all but perhaps the smallest craft (see Chapter 3 for details).

Weather tools—The principle weather predicting tools are a weather radio, barometer, and weatherfax on an offshore boat (see Chapter 8). A cruising boat in foggy areas sometimes carries a sling psychrometer which gauges relative humidity and dew point thus indicating the likelihood of fog.

Transmitting radio—A radio/telephone detracts from privacy and peacefulness (there is a need to monitor emergency frequencies), but there is no doubt that a VHF radio (for short range) or marine single sideband (for long range) provides the ability to call for help. Even if transmitters are installed, however, every offshore boat should carry at least one EPIRB (emergency position-indicating radio beacon, a portable device that sends out emergency signals). Chapter 7 provides more details.

Radar reflector—Every passagemaker needs a radar reflector, originally an octahedral device with right angled metal plates (now often enclosed in a plastic container), that may be hung in the rigging to improve visibility to vessels using radar.

Lee cloths or bunk boards—These are cloths or boards secured at the sides of bunks to prevent the crew from rolling out. They are particularly important on monohull sailboats that heel.

Safety harnesses—These are needed especially at night on offshore sailboats. The best harness consists of a wide safety belt with shoulder straps and tether line with locking snaphooks at each end. One end snaps to a strong point on the boat, and the other end snaps to the wearer's safety belt so that the wearer can release him- or herself if held underwater. Seagoing craft are often equipped with jacklines (ropes, wires, or preferably heavy tapes running fore and aft along the deck or cabin trunk to which safety harness tethers can be snapped to permit travel without the need of unhooking). A blue-water boat also needs a proper safety belt for the cook—one that will prevent falling against as well as away from the stove.

Life raft—Any sinkable vessel that goes far offshore should be equipped with a life raft (or rafts) large enough to accommodate the entire crew. Highly desirable or essential

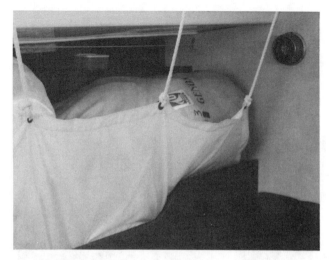

Fig. 1-9. Lee cloth on a pilot berth

features for an inflatable raft are: a fiberglass storage canister, a canopy for crew protection, double bottom, at least two separate air chambers, automatic CO_2 inflation, and an ample water bag or pockets under the raft's bottom to provide stability. Life raft supplies (either stowed inside the raft or in a separate emergency grab bag) should include: a sea anchor, inflation pump, repair kit, first aid kit, EPIRB, emergency food, plenty of drinking water, flares, whistle/horn, and flashlight.

Storm sails—Every sailboat that ventures into exposed waters needs heavy weather sails (these will be described in Chapter 2).

Sea Anchor—In my opinion, most vessels going offshore, especially those without a high range of stability, need a sea anchor or drogue (these will be discussed in Chapter 8).

Fig. 1-10. Safety harness with tether line shackled to pedestal

Fig. 1-11. A life raft and fiberglass canister stowed under the bridge deck on a Navy 44 (Photograph by William E. Brooks, III)

There are other important items primarily for crew comfort, such as dodgers (folding companionway shelters), Bimini tops (folding sun shelters), and weather cloths (cloth strips secured to the life lines to protect against spray); but the items listed in this chapter cover the essentials in safety gear.

2. Ropes, Rigging, and Sails

The myriad of halyards, lifts, braces, and outhauls around the foremast formed a cat's cradle that took a smart man to find his way around on a dark night. —John Parkinson, Jr.

In the days of "iron men and wooden ships" every seaman had to find his way around such cat's cradles described by nautical historian John Parkinson. With the simpler rigging of today, the demands on a seaman are not so great, but even so, a competent sailor must know the rigging and sails, and even the powerboat skipper needs to have some rudimentary knowledge of ropes. Ropes are not only used for the control of sails, but also for flag halyards, lashings, heaving lines, dock lines, anchor rodes, tow ropes, mooring lines, and other purposes.

ROPES

As a general rule, ropes are termed lines when put to a specific use on a boat. There are said to be seven exceptions to this rule, where ropes used for a specific purpose are referred to as ropes. Those exceptions are foot rope (under a yard), top rope (to stay the head of a mast), wheel rope (on a steering wheel), back rope (on a dolphin striker under a bowsprit), man rope (on a gangway), bolt rope (at the edge of a sail), and bell rope (to ring the bell). The

32

latter three ropes are about the only ones commonly used by modern boaters.

Fiber ropes (as opposed to wire ropes) are mostly made of synthetic materials today: nylon, polyester (Dacron), polypropylene, aramid (Kevlar), and polyethylene (Spectra and Dyneema). Construction normally consists of twisting or braiding the fibers, but sometimes the interior fibers are run parallel to each other for stretch resistance. Most modern braided ropes have external covers and internal cores. Quite often the covers and cores are of different materials. The following are some abbreviated comments about ropes and their use on board a boat.

— Nylon is somewhat elastic and so is ideal for dock and mooring lines, anchor rodes, tow ropes, and safety tethers.

— Dacron is an economical, low-stretch, high-strength fiber with good resistance to chafe and weather. It is most suitable for sheets and most halyards or for rope tails on wire halyards aboard cruising boats and daysailers.

— Polypropylene is far inferior in strength to nylon or Dacron, but it is light and will float. About its only practical use is for crew overboard heaving lines or lightweight tails that will take modest strains on racing craft.

— Kevlar is highly stretch resistant, tremendously strong, and has had a place on racing boats, but it has serious drawbacks in susceptibility to fatigue from sharp bending and knotting and poor resistance to chafe and ultraviolet (sun) exposure. The chafe and sun problems are alleviated when Kevlar is used as a core provided with a Dacron cover. An extra large sheave with a flat groove is needed for a Kevlar line.

— Spectra and Dyneema also have tremendous strength and are more resistant to sun, chafe, and sharp bending

than Kevlar, but they are subject to creep (gradual elongation after a long period of tension). At least one producer
of Dyneema claims that the creep problem has been alleviated with the use of oils, needed during extrusion, that
later evaporate.

— Composite rope, using a combination of Kevlar and
Spectra or Dyneema with a cover of Dacron, seems a good
compromise for the halyards on racers or cruising boats
whose skippers want to do away with all-wire halyards
and the hazards of reel winches (see Chapter 3) or the
avoidance of wire-to-rope splices.

— Three strand twisted rope is somewhat more stretchy
than braided line, but it is easier to splice and coil without
kinking and is more durable in chocks than cored lines
with covers.

— Most twisted rope used on a boat is laid right-handed
(fibers are twisted to the right to form yarns, yarns to the
left to form strands, and strands to the right to form the
rope). Such line should be coiled clockwise in circular
loops to prevent kinking. Normally, braided line is coiled
in figure 8 loops to avoid kinks.

— A badly kinked line can be towed from a moving boat to
untwist it, but great care must be taken to see that it will
not foul the propeller when under power.

— When choosing the size of rope for a sheet, determine
the maximum load expected and consult a rope catalog to
determine tensile strength for various diameters of line.
As a general rule, do not exceed 20 percent of the tensile
strength for a safe working load. Maximum load can be
figured with the formula: Load in pounds = $.00431 \times A \times V^2$ (A being the sail area in square feet and V the wind
velocity in knots).

— In determining the correct diameter of rope, considerations other than strength are: a size that allows firm hand

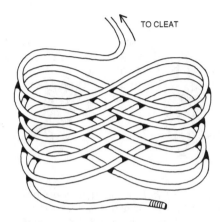

TO CLEAT

Fig. 2-1. A figure-8 coil

gripping; ability to withstand chafe; and the proper match-
ing of size to fittings such as blocks, cleats, chocks, and
winches which will service the line.

— Do what you can to prevent lines from chafing. Use
fairleads, smooth chocks, large blocks, chafe guards, and
shroud rollers (to protect sheets).

— Cleating on a conventional cleat with horns is properly
done by making a round turn around the cleat first before
beginning the crisscross wraps. As a general rule, cleated
halyards should be hitched (the cleating finished with a
half hitch) for security when synthetic line is used, but
sheets should not be hitched unless a slippery hitch is
used (slippery hitches are those used when tying a shoe
so that the knot may be quickly untied by pulling the ends
of the lace).

— Unraveled ends of lines, often called cow's tails, are not
just a sign of sloppy seamanship, but a cause for concern

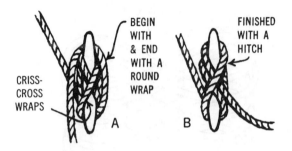

Fig. 2-2. Methods of belaying on a conventional cleat. Method B may be used on a halyard but a sheet should never be hitched unless a slippery hitch is used.

that the line will foul, jam, or become unlaid. To prevent cow's tails the ends of lines should be whipped with waxed thread or otherwise bound. The most secure type of whipping is made with a sailmaker's needle. In this method the thread is pushed through the rope, wound numerous times around the rope, and then the winding is held securely by inserting the needle through the rope and repeatedly running the thread back and forth across the winding (inserting the needle after each crossing) following the lay of the line. The ends of braided lines are often bound with heat-shrunk plastic sleeves or plastic dip. Small synthetic lines can have their ends sealed by melting them with flame or other heat.

—When it is desirable to put a permanent eye in the end of a line or to secure the line permanently to a fitting, an eye splice should be used since it weakens the line much less than most knots. The making of this splice with twisted line is described in the Cornell Boaters Library book called *Handbook of Knots* by Raoul Graumont. The

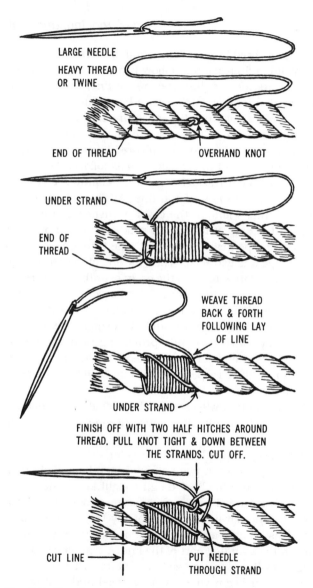

LARGE NEEDLE
HEAVY THREAD
OR TWINE

END OF THREAD   OVERHAND KNOT

UNDER STRAND

END OF
THREAD

WEAVE THREAD
BACK & FORTH
FOLLOWING LAY
OF LINE

UNDER STRAND

FINISH OFF WITH TWO HALF HITCHES AROUND
THREAD. PULL KNOT TIGHT & DOWN BETWEEN
THE STRANDS. CUT OFF.

CUT LINE →   PUT NEEDLE
                    THROUGH STRAND

Fig. 2-3. Needle whipping a line

splicing of cored braided line requires two special tools, a hollow fid (a dull-pointed hollow tube of narrow diameter appropriate for the diameter of the line) and a pusher (similar to a long ice pick with a blunt end). Specific instructions for making the splice are normally provided with the tools when they are purchased. The simplified principle of the procedure for a cored line (with a braided center rope and a braided cover) is as follows: The center rope is extracted through the cover slightly over two fid lengths from the end of the line. At about half the extracted center's length, the cover is turned and inserted through the core of the center rope and pulled out from the center rope near the original hole through which the center rope was extracted. Then the end of the center rope is turned and inserted into the cover near the hole through which the cover exits from the center rope. The latter is pushed through the cover and its end exits directly opposite the exit of the cover through the center rope. We then have an eye with two ends projecting near the splice. These exposed ends are unravelled, cut into a taper, and worked into their respective holes by "milking" the cover of the line.

— Eye splices that will receive a lot of chafe such as those in anchor rodes or dinghy painters need metal thimbles in their centers.

— The most commonly used knots for the boater are the bowline, square knot, two half hitches, rolling hitch, buntline hitch, clove hitch, and figure eight knot. These (and many others) are shown in the aforementioned *Handbook of Knots*. The bowline is undoubtedly the most essential knot. It is reliable and will not jam, but tying it requires slack in the standing part of the line. A seamanlike way of tying a bowline is to capsize it, i.e., start with an overhand knot (as you begin when tying a shoe) and pull on the

line's end so that a loop is formed in the standing part.
Then pass the end around the standing part and back
through the loop.When there is strain on the standing
part so that a loop cannot be formed, the line can be
passed around an object and secured to its standing part
with two (or more) half hitches or a buntline hitch. The
latter knot is more secure and compact but is subject to
jamming. It is a good one for securing halyards or guys to
shackles. A close relative of the bowline, the sheet bend is
used to join two lines. The rolling hitch is useful when you
want to secure a line to a wire or fiber rope or spar without the line sliding along the rope or spar. When temporarily securing a dock line to a post or pile a clove hitch is
often used, but this knot lacks security unless a half hitch
is put around the standing part of the line. A better
knot for this purpose, allowing more security and control, is the backhanded hitch shown in the illustration.
The square knot is most often used to tie reef points and
sail stops. Figure eight knots prevent the ends of lines
from running through blocks or other fittings.

RIGGING AND RELATED FITTINGS

There are two general types of rigging, standing and running. The latter runs or moves and is used to control sails,

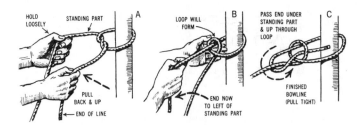

Fig. 2-4. Capsizing method of tying a bowline

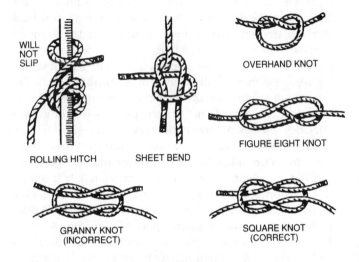

WILL NOT SLIP

ROLLING HITCH

SHEET BEND

OVERHAND KNOT

FIGURE EIGHT KNOT

GRANNY KNOT (INCORRECT)

SQUARE KNOT (CORRECT)

Fig. 2-5. Commonly used knots. Please note that the granny knot is often mistakenly used in place of the square knot.

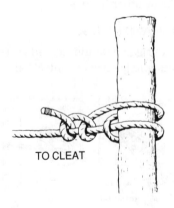

TO CLEAT

Fig. 2-6. Backhanded hitch

while the former is fixed or semifixed and is used primarily to support masts but may also carry sails. Running rigging, consisting of sheets, halyards, guys, downhauls, etc., is comprised mostly of fiber rope, although flexible wire rope often is used for halyards. Standing rigging, which includes stays and shrouds (side stays), normally is made of wire rope, but solid rod rigging is more often used by modern racers.

Running Rigging & Fittings

— Most sheets and fiber rope halyards should be tied to their shackles or sail so that the line periodically can be turned end-for-end to increase longevity. Also, splices can be pulled into blocks and possibly jam or be weakened.

— Snap shackles on jib sheets can open when the sail is flapping violently, and they have caused injuries to crew on the foredeck. It is far better to tie the sheet to the jib's clew grommet with a bowline.

— Never go aloft in a bosun's chair secured with a snap shackle unless the shackle's pin is tied or taped closed.

— Spinnaker sheets and guys, however, should be secured to clews with wide-opening snap shackles (see illustration) for quick release. There should be a short lanyard secured to the ring of the shackle's pull-pin as illustrated.

— As a general rule, spinnaker sheets and guys should be twice the overall length of boat.

— The power of a tackle (system of blocks and line for mechanical advantage) is measured by the number of rope parts at the non-fixed or movable end. The degree of power is designated by the number of parts (for example, a three-part or four-part tackle).

— Fiber rope halyards should be the low stretch type (perhaps the composite rope mentioned earlier) except for

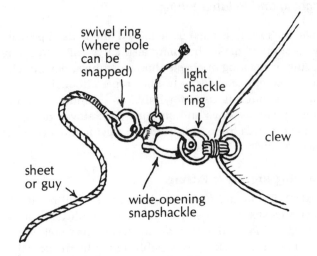

Fig. 2-7. Wide-opening snap shackle

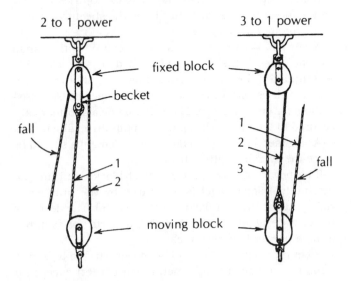

Fig. 2-8. Tackle power

spinnaker halyards which need a little give for shock absorption. Twisted Dacron supplies sufficient give for the considerable shock of a collapsed spinnaker which suddenly fills with wind.

—Wire halyards are often given rope tails, especially those used for jibs, to allow easy handling and cleating. A tail is joined to the wire part of the halyard with a wire-to-rope splice. (Although this splice is very strong when well made by an experienced rigger, it is not the best practice to leave a sail under heavy strain supported by a wire-to-rope splice.) The wire part of the halyard should be sufficiently long to wrap three or preferably four times around a large diameter winch after sail is hoisted. For jibs with short luffs, this means that tack and/or head pendants should be added. These lengths of wire serve to extend the wire halyard far enough so that it can reach and adequately wrap around the winch.

—All-wire halyards (without tails) are sometimes used for mainsails, and these are serviced by reel winches, those that wind up and store halyards on their drums similar to fishing reels. Such winches can be very dangerous unless the operator knows how to handle them. The principle risk is in being struck by the spinning handle after the brake has been released. Acquire reel winches with screw toggle brakes that allow gradual easing, otherwise use a winch wheel instead of a handle. Rules for safe handling are: Always remove the handle before lowering sail, hoist with the brake on, grip the handle firmly, keep head and other parts of your body away from handle, never leave handles inserted, ease tension on the downhaul before lowering, and never oil the brake band.

—Use flexible wire such as 7 × 19 (seven strands having 19 wires each) for halyards and use sheaves of large diameter, at least twenty times the diameter of the halyard.

Fig. 2-9. Winch wheel

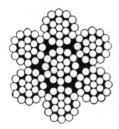

Fig. 2-10. Construction of 7 × 19 wire rope

— See that the halyard is marked to align with a mast mark to avoid damaging the end of the halyard or fittings from overhoisting.

— Sheet winches, which take only four or five wraps of line, are not so dangerous, but they too should be carefully handled. They need periodic (preferably at least once a year) lubrication with light oil which will not become gummy and hamper the operation of pawls and springs. When first beginning to tail a sheet (hauling in on the line after it has been wrapped around the winch) don't put too many turns on the drum before the winch handle is inserted, as there is some risk of a jamming override. Two or possibly three wraps are enough until just before the winch handle is inserted. Also, keep the sheet at least 90 degrees to the winch axis to prevent an override and the fall (hauling part) of the line approximately 90 degrees as illustrated to keep the line from slipping off the drum. When slacking off a sheet under strain take the wraps off carefully while keeping a strain on the fall. Use the ball of your free hand to apply some friction to the few remaining wraps and keep your fingers away from the swallow (where the fall meets the drum).

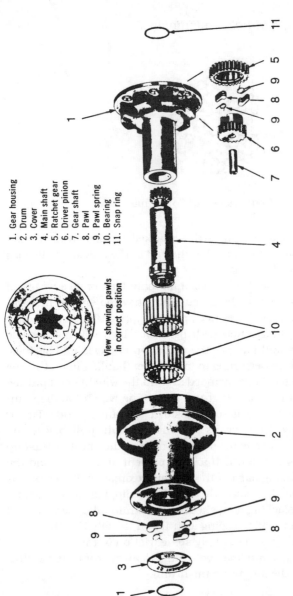

1. Gear housing
2. Drum
3. Cover
4. Main shaft
5. Ratchet gear
6. Driver pinion
7. Gear shaft
8. Pawl
9. Pawl spring
10. Bearing
11. Snap ring

View showing pawls in correct position

Fig. 2-11. Exploded view of Barient sheet winch (From Sailboat Maintenance by Eric Jorgensen)

— Common mistakes in handling sheet winches are: Not clearing the windward sheet before tacking, wrapping the sheet around the drum in the wrong direction (wrap clockwise on most winches), and uncleating the line before cranking when trimming (this merely wastes time).

— It is especially important to keep fingers away from the swallow of a block, cleat, or chock when a line under strain is being slacked, as a finger could be pulled into the fitting and be seriously injured.

— Blocks must allow fairleading so that the line under strain leads almost directly away from the sheave without bearing against the checks. Otherwise the line will chafe and the block could be damaged. Fairleading usually can be assured with a swiveling head or simply by adding an extra shackle to allow the block to turn in the direction of pull.

— Don't use snatch blocks as lead blocks for storm jibs as they can shake open.

— See that your cleats are mounted at a slight angle to the direction of the line's pull (from 10 to 30 degrees) to avoid having the line jam when uncleating.

— See that turning blocks (those which change direction of a line's pull) are extra strong and are securely through-bolted with backing plates. Avoid the use of cast aluminum blocks (or other fittings) which may have internal flaws.

Standing Rigging and Fittings

—A foremost consideration regarding standing rigging is the prevention of metal fatigue (work hardening) from constant flexing of metal fittings. Be sure that chain-plates and tangs are bent at the proper angle to align with the shrouds. An imaginary straight line extending from the ends of each shroud should exactly follow the angle of the chain-plate (lower-end attachment) and the tang (upper-end attachment). Misalignment will cause flexing of the metal parts as the shroud alternately becomes loaded and unloaded when changing tacks.

— Use toggles at the lower ends of shrouds and especially stays which carry sails. Toggles act as universal joints and help prevent fatigue. Stays that carry long luff sails also need toggling action at the top as well as at the bottom of the stay.

— Rigging should be tuned to hold the mast straight when viewed from the fore and aft direction. Normally, this requires that the upper shrouds passing over spreaders are carried more taut than the lowers.

— Shrouds should join the mast at an angle of at least 10 degrees, as a smaller angle causes excessive compression loading. The angle can be increased by lengthening the spreaders.

— Mastheads may be bent aft (usually by tightening the permanent backstay) to a more or less limited extent in order to flatten the mainsail, thereby increasing its efficiency in a fresh breeze. Fractional rigged boats (with the jib stay not going to the masthead) having flexible rigs and full mainsails use mast bend to the greatest extent. Bend should be no more than moderate with masthead rigs (where the jib stay goes to the masthead).

— The rigging on cruisers and offshore sailers should be kept only moderately taut—not so slack as to allow mast movement nor so taut as to strain the hull or rig.

— Use flexible wire such as 7×7 construction (seven strands having seven wires each) when rigging is spliced. For minimal stretch use rod (preferably Nitronic 50 stainless steel or MP 35 cobalt) on racers or, for cruisers and offshore sailers, 1×19 wire (one strand of nineteen wires).

— Dyform 1×19, with minimal space between wires, provides less stretch than standard nonflexible 1×19 cable.

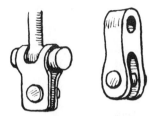

Fig. 2-12. Rigging toggles

Fig. 2-13. Construction of standard 1 × 19 wire rope (left) *and Dyform 1 × 19* (right)

—All rigging pins in oversized holes should have bushings to avoid point loading.

—Avoid the use of closed turnbuckles having locknuts, as one can't see how far the threaded shanks are screwed into the barrels, and locknuts put extra strain on the threads.

—Be cautious in the use of a turnbuckle with an adjustable center screw, as some shanks have broken immediately above or below the center screw.

—Keep turnbuckles well lubricated (preferably greased with lanolin) to avoid galling of threads. Be wary of looseness of shanks in barrels and replace at once any turnbuckle that shows evidence of peeling threads.

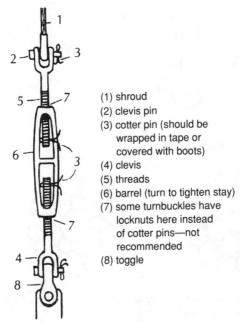

(1) shroud
(2) clevis pin
(3) cotter pin (should be
    wrapped in tape or
    covered with boots)
(4) clevis
(5) threads
(6) barrel (turn to tighten stay)
(7) some turnbuckles have
    locknuts here instead
    of cotter pins—not
    recommended
(8) toggle

Fig. 2-14. Open barrel turnbuckles

—Spreader tips must be securely clamped or lashed to the shrouds, as a spreader that slips could cause a dismasting. The angle between the top of a spreader and its shroud should exactly equal the angle between the bottom of the spreader and the shroud. Wood spreaders should have a ferrule (metal band) at the tip to prevent splitting and tips should be wrapped in felt or have a roller or boot to protect sails.
—Potentially vulnerable parts of standing rigging are terminal fittings or connection eyes or forks at the ends of stays or shrouds. Forks are more vulnerable to failure,

and so eyes should be used whenever possible. Terminal fittings are normally swaged, squeezed onto the wire with a swaging machine, but some terminals (such as Norseman) are mechanically fastened. The latter can be disassembled and internally inspected and are replaceable without elaborate equipment. They are often preferred by long-distance cruising sailors, especially those in tropical waters where swaged fittings seem to deteriorate more rapidly. Prudent seamanship requires regular inspection of all terminal fittings. Carefully look for cracks in the terminals, and examine the cable for broken wires where it emerges from the fitting.

— Double tang plates supporting an eye terminal fitting should be equally bent to avoid flexing one plate.

— Clevis pins that lock fittings to rigging should be held in place with split cotter pins. Avoid the use of circular cotters (ring dings) that can work loose. Cotter pins should be regularly inspected and taped or covered with boots to avoid tearing sails.

— If rod rigging is used on long distance cruisers, it is a good idea to use fatigue-indicating fittings or warning pieces (as produced by Navtec) to give warning of sudden failure. Wire rigging normally gives sufficient warning, because it tends to break one wire at a time.

— On offshore boats avoid the use of T terminals (T-shaped fittings that fit into a mast slot) as they are more subject to fatigue.

SAILS

This books will not attempt to deal with sophisticated, "grand prix" type racing sails but will concentrate on those used for cruising, daysailing, and informal club racing. The accompanying illustration shows the basic sails

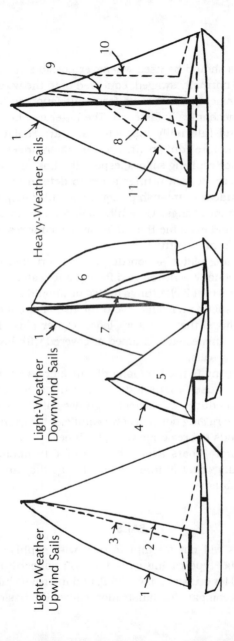

Light-Weather Upwind Sails

Light-Weather Downwind Sails

Heavy-Weather Sails

1—mainsail. 2—no. 1 genoa. 3—drifter or reacher (sheeted to main boom or deck). 4—mizzen. 5—mizzen staysail. 6—spinnaker. 7—spinnaker staysail. 8—no. 2 genoa. 9— working jib. 10—storm jib or spitfire. 11—storm trysail (sheeted to main boom or deck).

Fig. 2-15. Basic sails for all weather

used for sailing upwind and downwind in light weather and those used in heavy weather. Not all of these sails are really needed, but they can add speed or safety and make sailing more interesting. The least essential sails of those illustrated are the spinnaker staysail (carried with a spinnaker) and the mizzen staysail shown on the drawing of the yawl. The most essential sails are the mainsail, of course, mizzen on a yawl or ketch, working jib, and a number 1 (large) genoa jib for power in light to moderate winds. For long cruises the drifter/reacher is a very useful sail, as it adds considerable power in reaching conditions in very light to medium winds. Its high-cut foot prevents excessive twist, permits trimming to the end of the main boom (as illustrated) when this is desirable, and allows good visibility. The number 2 genoa is a useful sail for fresh winds when the boat is overpowered by the number 1 but underpowered by the small working jib. Storm sails, the trysail and spitfire, are for very heavy weather and are important for boats venturing far offshore. Spinnakers are used mostly for racing and can be tricky to handle; but they are fun and add lots of power when sailing off the wind on almost any boat. An asymmetrical spinnaker (with one leech longer than the other) can be carried without a pole.

Materials
As with rope, sails are now made of a variety of synthetic materials: nylon, Dacron, Kevlar, Mylar, Spectra, and even carbon fiber.

— Nylon, which can be obtained in very light weights, is somewhat elastic and so is only suitable for a few sails used when sailing downwind, especially for spinnakers.

— Dacron (polyester) is the most versatile material and is best in terms of durability, reasonable stretch resistance, and economy for most cruising boats and daysailers.

Fig. 2-16. An asymmetrical spinnaker carried without a pole (Courtesy Jack Quinn)

—Kevlar, Mylar, Spectra, and carbon fiber are highly re-sistant to stretch, but are expensive and usually require very elaborate construction. Sails of these materials are often stiff and must be folded or preferably rolled rather than stuffed into a bag. They are most appropriate for racing boats that need very stable sails and minimal weight aloft. At present, carbon fiber is used in America's Cup composite sails and is not yet for the average boater.

—Kevlar, a composite cloth usually combined with Da-cron, is most often used for sail reinforcement, especially at clews and leeches. The material has high stretch resis-tance but is subject to fatigue from constant bending or flapping.

—Mylar is a polyester film that avoids bias elongation (stretching in a direction that is diagonal to the weave), and it is normally laminated to Dacron or used to sand-wich a substrate called scrim. Its greatest drawbacks are possible delamination or tearing and stiffness, but it can be suitable in relatively soft form for roller furling jibs.

—Spectra, a more recently developed polyethylene fiber, is less subject to fatigue than Kevlar but is prone to creep (see page 34). Large cruisers sometimes use Spectra for their mainsails.

Construction

—A primary consideration in sail construction is the elimination or minimization of bias elongation, where the loading is diagonal to the weave causing the threads to realign and form diamond rather than square patterns. The attempt is made to align cloth panels so that the stress runs parallel with the threads.

—Although the construction patterns of modern racing sails often appear very complicated, all sails are based on four basic systems of cloth orientation or combinations thereof: vertical, horizontal or crosscut, miter, and radial.

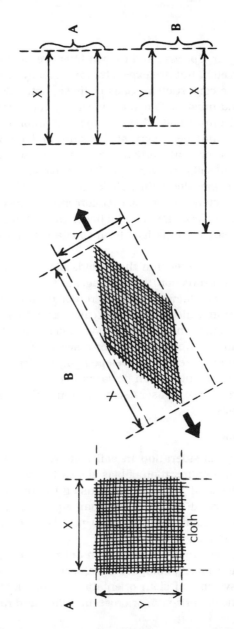

Fig. 2-17. Bias elongation

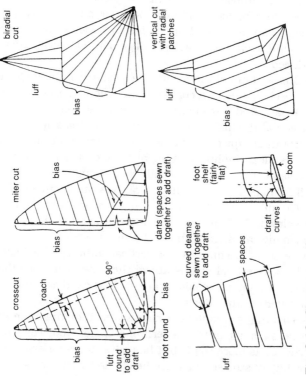

Fig. 2-18. Common sail cuts

—Vertically cut sails, with seams running parallel to the leech, follow an old system that is resurging today. Although the nearly vertical seams somewhat interrupt the flow of air across the sail, they prevent the sail from splitting horizontally. This construction is often suitable for roller jibs (those that roll up on their luff) that will be sailed in a reefed condition, because panels of varying weight can be used. Progressively heavier cloth is used from luff to clew, so that the sail gets heavier as its area is reduced.

—Crosscut orientation, with the seams at right angles to the leech, is the most common construction, especially for mainsails and mizzens. It is economical, minimizes bias stretch at the highly stressed leech, and the seams minimally interrupt the air flow. Furthermore, because the seams meet the luff on a slight bias, draft (curvature) of the sail can be adjusted easily by altering tension of the luff for maximum efficiency in various wind conditions.

—The miter cut consists of a miter seam running from the clew to luff, meeting the latter at about right angles. Normally, all seams above the miter are crosscut and those below are more or less vertical, although the Scotch cut uses vertical seams above the miter. Jibs or other sails not attached to booms are the best candidates suited for miter constructions.

—Sails that are radial cut have seams radiating from the corners similar to the pattern of a spider web. This construction is more costly but has advantages for sails that are highly stressed at their heads and clews, especially spinnakers and jibs. Common forms of this cut are the triradial for spinnakers and biradial (with the seams radiating from head and clew) for jibs. Some jibs are merely given radial corner patches (reinforcements) as illustrated.

Sail Tips

—An old formula for determining the cloth weight (in ounces) of a Dacron cruising mainsail is to add the boat's overall length to the sail's luff length and divide by ten. This might seems a bit heavy considering the stability of cloth today, but it is best to err on the heavy side if the boat will be sailed offshore.

—The use of soft, unresinated cloth in a crusing sail will reduce the difficulties of handling and increase the life of the sail but at some cost in cloth stability and a need for more frequent adjustments.

—Draft or camber (fore and aft curvature in a sail) should be fairly deep and near the sail's middle in light airs and when sailing downwind, as shown in the accompanying illustration. For upwind sailing and in fresher winds the point of maximum draft needs to be farther forward and the sail should be flatter.

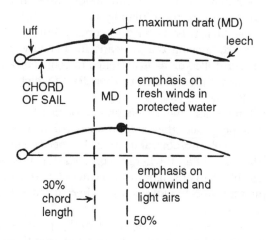

Fig. 2-19. Sail draft

—Draft can be adjusted particularly with a soft sail by tightening or slacking the halyard and outhaul. A tight halyard flattens the luff and pulls the draft forward. A tight outhaul flattens the sail at its foot.

—Jib draft can be increased for more power in light winds by slightly slacking off the jibstay. In many cases jibstay tension can be controlled by adjusting the backstay.

—A taut jibstay is needed for fresh winds and especially when beating to windward so that the boat can point high (sail closer to the wind).

—Jib sheet leads (usually consisting of a block attached to a slide on a track) should be adjusted to keep approximately equal tension on the foot and leech. Push the lead further forward and there is greater tension on the leech; push it further aft and there is greater tension on the foot.

—Sail twist is the difference in trim angles between the head and foot. Some twist is needed, but if the top of the sail definitely flaps before the bottom when heading up toward the wind, there usually is too much twist. With boomless jibs, twist is hard to control, but some can be removed by moving the jib leads further forward. Twist can be controlled on sails attached to booms by adjusting the boom vang (a tackle or other device which pulls the boom down).

—Watch out for chafe. Sails should be fitted with protective patches where they continuously rub against the rigging. Particularly vulnerable areas that need chafe patches are the leech of a jib where it contacts the spreader tips, the leech of a mainsail or mizzen where it is rubbed by the topping lift, and the foot of a jib where it crosses the lifelines.

—Don't allow sails to flog for lengthy periods of time, especially in fresh winds, as this will break threads and lessen the life of the sail.

Fig. 2-20. Dark areas on the sail cloth are chafe patches to
protect against the spreaders and lower shrouds

— Have your sails double- or preferably triple-stitched, and specify dark stitching which better resists sun rot and allows easy detection of broken stitching.

— Minimize leech flutter by moving leads further forward, tightening the leech line, decreasing the sail's roach (re-cutting the sail to decrease the outward curvature of the leech), or adding battens.

— See that your battens are strong (preferably made of solid plastic, carbon fiber, or fiberglass) unwarped, and smooth (so as not to chafe the sails). Batten ends need soft plastic protectors to avoid chafe. Solid tubes are often best for full-length battens.

— Battenless sails may need a hollow leech or at least no roach to prevent leech curling or flutter.

— Avoid the use of a heavy D ring at the clew of a jib, as it can strike a crew member when the sail is flapping.

— See that your sails are provided with an efficient means of reefing. A simple modern method of reducing the area of a boomed sail is with jiffy reefing. This method will be explained in Chapter 8. It is customary to have two reefs for the mainsail of a cruising boat with each reef reducing the area by 25 percent. When there is only one reef it should reduce the area by about one third, and when this reduction is insufficient, a storm trysail should be used.

— A very popular means of reducing a jib's area is with roller furling, whereby the sail is rolled up on its own luff in the manner of a roller window shade. This method is convenient and quick, but it sacrifices optimal shape and allows no means of tensioning the luff. A roller jib carried in reefed condition should be cut extra flat, and it needs a means of reducing draft such as having a foam padded luff and/or a double swivel furling drum, or North Sails' AEROLUFF system which starts rolling the jib in the mid-dle of its luff.

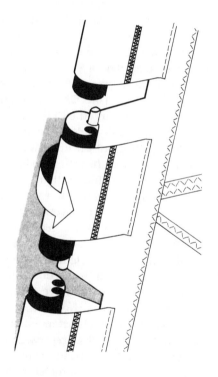

Fig. 2-21. North Sails' AEROLUFF system of reducing draft (Courtesy North Sails)

—When unrolling a roller sail, keep some tension on the furling line (perhaps two turns of the furling line on a winch) to prevent an override on the drum under the tack of the sail. Likewise, keep a little tension on the sheet when hauling on the furling line to get a tight furl.

—Heavy weather sails that may have to be changed or lowered need a positive means of attachment to the stay or mast with slides or hanks.

—When reducing sail keep the boat in balance. This means that the total center of effort (TCE) of the sails should slightly lead (be forward of) the center of lateral resistance (CLR) of the hull. The TCE is the geometric center of the sail plan's profile, and the CLR is considered the geometric center of the hull's underwater profile. The latter can be found by cutting out the underwater profile and hanging it from a pin so that the waterline is horizontal as shown in the accompanying illustration. The center of a triangle sail is found by bisecting each side and drawing straight lines from each point of bisection to the opposite corner. These lines intersect at the geometric center as illustrated. To find the TCE of a sloop, join the centers of the jib and mainsail with a straight line and locate the TCE on the connecting line in proportion to the areas of the two sails. The illustration shows vertical lines at the CEs in proportion to the areas. Notice that the vertical representing the mainsail's area is extended upward above the jib's center, while the vertical representing the jib's area is drawn down from the mainsail's center. A line connecting the ends of the verticals intersects the line connecting the individual centers at the TCE.

—A good general rule for the typical modern cruiser is that the TCE should lead the CLR by about 15 percent of the waterline length so that a boat will not have excessive

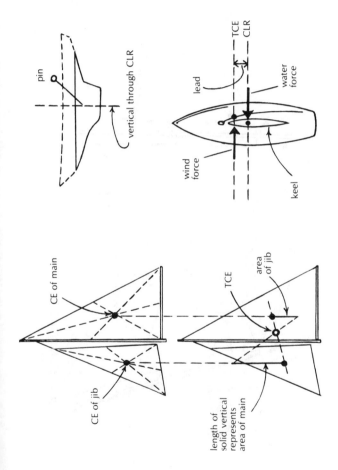

Fig. 2-22. Centers of effort and lateral resistance

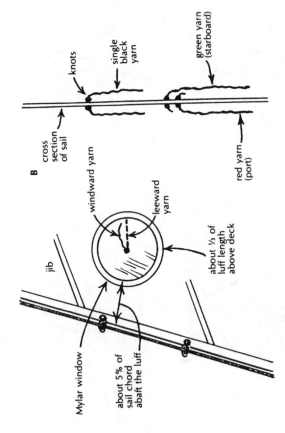

B

cross section of sail

knots

single black yarn

green yarn (starboard)

red yarn (port)

windward yarn

leeward yarn

about ⅓ of luff length above deck

jib

Mylar window

about 5% of sail chord abaft the luff

Fig. 2-23. Luff telltales

weather helm (a strong tendency to turn into the wind) nor lee helm (a tendency to turn away from the wind).

— Never tolerate a lee helm, especially in a capsizable centerboard boat. If your boat tends to turn away from the wind, increase the sail area aft or rake the mast (make it lean aft) to reduce lead by moving the CE aft. Weather helm can be relieved by reducing rake and heel and increasing sail area forward.

— See that your jibs are fitted with telltales (ribbons or yarns fastened to the sail's luff at about a third of the luff length above the tack. Yarns are usually threaded through the sail about 5 percent of the chord length (straight line distance from luff to leech) abaft the jib stay. A Mylar window, as illustrated, allows easy viewing of the yarns on both sides of the sail. The yarns are usually black, but some sailors prefer green on the starboard side and red on the port side. A great aid to proper sail trim, telltales should be kept flowing directly aft (rather than fluttering or twirling) on each side of the sail. Twirling on the leeward side indicates the sail is stalled, and the helmsman should either head up closer to the wind or slack the sheet. A telltale fluttering on the windward side indicates that the boat is being sailed too close to the wind or else the sheet should be trimmed.

— When luff length permits, there should be a tack pendant (short wire strop at the tack) to raise the jib's foot in order to keep it clear of the bow wave and permit better visibility for the helmsman and crew in the cockpit.

3. Getting Underway, Docking, and Securing

The sloop naturally rounded in the wind, and just ranging ahead, laid her cheek against a mooring-pile at the windward corner of the wharf, so quietly, after all, that she would not have broken an egg.
— *Captain Joshua Slocum*

Seamanship is often judged by the skill with which a skipper can handle a vessel around a pier or in a crowded harbor when getting underway or returning to port. It is far from easy to dock a heavy boat under sail, especially singlehandedly, and even a masterful seaman such as Josh Slocum, the first person to sail around the world alone, could have problems, for after his above-quoted successful landing in a crowded harbor he later "scratched the paint off an old fine-weather craft in the fairway." One must avoid taking unnecessary chances, plan ahead, and understand the various forces that act on the boat.

FORCES AT WORK

The primary force of concern to a sailboat is, of course, the wind. Even a high freeboard powerboat, however, is affected by windage, the air drag caused by parts of the boat (topsides, cabins, and even rigging) exposed to the wind. Obviously, the stronger the wind, the greater the windage. Another important factor is draft, or depth of the vessel's underbody. Boats with minimal appendages and shallow draft are most affected by their windage.

Another force to be reckoned with is the current, or horizontal movement of the water. This can be a significant factor in some areas, but most protected harbors don't have strong current. Before getting underway or returning to a mooring or dock always check the current. It can be read by watching the flow of water past a stationary object such as a piling or mooring.

Still other forces are the ones artificially created with sails, the vessel's engine, or warping or kedging with lines (warping is moving a boat with lines normally attached to a pile or pier, while kedging is moving the boat by hauling in on her anchor line). Just how the boat will move when subjected to the various forces will depend not only on her windage and draft but also on her size, weight, underwater shape, propeller, rudder, and rig. Weight affects the boat's momentum or the amount of way she carries (the distance she will coast when power is cut). The heavier the boat, the more way she carries and the more difficult it will be to make her stop.

Steering characteristics are affected by the hull's underwater shape. Boats with long keels normally have a steady helm but slower response and larger turning circles as compared to boats with short keels. When the forefoot (forward part of the hull underwater) is cutaway and the keel has drag (greater depth at its after end), the bow will tend to blow off or be turned downwind by the breeze.

Rudder effectiveness depends on its size, depth, location, type (see Chapter 1), and proximity of the propeller. When prop wash (water flow created by the propeller) is directed against the rudder blade, steering is much more effective. In general, the larger and deeper the rudder and the further aft it is located, the more effective it will be, but only if the boat is moving. A wayless (dead in the water) boat cannot be steered, although on some small boats the rudder can be used to scull the stern around (by quickly turning the helm in one direction, then slowly in the other).

On some boats (not all) the propeller wheel effect is a significant force. Often less correctly called propeller torque, the wheel effect is caused by the turning propeller walking the stern to starboard or port. Remember that the port side is the left side when looking forward, and starboard is the right side. (Novices can think of the expression "A forward looking man has red port [wine] left.") The usual righthanded prop (turning clockwise) driving the boat ahead walks the stern to starboard. When going ahead think: righthand prop—right stern walk. Of course, the opposite would be true when going in reverse; the stern would be walked to the left. Two explanations for the wheel effect are illustrated. One shows that the prop operates in more solid (with less cavitation or aeration) water at the bottom of its rotation, and the other shows that there is less propeller pitch on one side than the other when the shaft is angled downward. The less usual lefthanded prop (turning counterclockwise) would walk the stern to the left when going ahead. Wheel effect is usually most pronounced when backing and when there is little or no way on the boat.

CHECKLIST FOR GETTING UNDERWAY

Every boat of any size should have a logbook or, more accurately, a ship's notebook that provides details on such matters as lock combinations, fuel and lube oil records, tank capacities, lead positions for various jibs, stowage locations for gear, needed repairs, seacock locations,

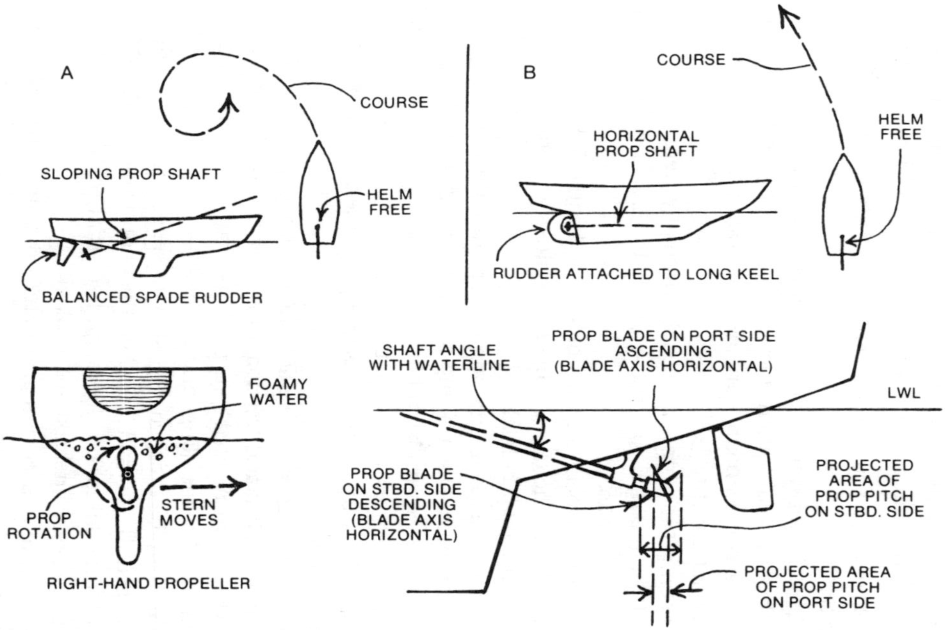
A
COURSE
SLOPING PROP SHAFT
HELM FREE
BALANCED SPADE RUDDER
B
COURSE
HORIZONTAL PROP SHAFT
HELM FREE
RUDDER ATTACHED TO LONG KEEL
FOAMY WATER
PROP ROTATION
STERN MOVES
RIGHT-HAND PROPELLER
SHAFT ANGLE WITH WATERLINE
PROP BLADE ON PORT SIDE ASCENDING (BLADE AXIS HORIZONTAL)
LWL
PROP BLADE ON STBD. SIDE DESCENDING (BLADE AXIS HORIZONTAL)
PROJECTED AREA OF PROP PITCH ON STBD. SIDE
PROJECTED AREA OF PROP PITCH ON PORT SIDE

Fig. 3-1. Propeller wheel effect

brand names of products used, compass deviation, operating instructions, and checklists. The following list is a reminder of what needs to be done before getting underway:

— Check the weather and wind (more about this in Chapter 8).

— Check personal gear (be properly garbed with the clothes and equipment mentioned in Chapter 1.)

— After going aboard, unlock and open all hatches to let the boat air out.

— Locate the ship's notebook (normally kept in a bookshelf or chart desk) and consult it when necessary for needed details.

— Open seacocks for the engine and head (WC). On a sailboat close seacocks on offcenter sinks that can overflow when the boat is heeled.

— Check the bilge and pump it dry in both the cabin and engine room. Don't pump oily water overboard.

— Remove covers from binnacle, winches, tiller, etc., and remove gilguys (lines that hold halyards away from the mast). Stow all these items in a permanent location (listed in notebook).

— Lower dodger and remove any cockpit covers to assure good visibility and freedom of movement for the crew.

— Break out needed gear such as cranks, winch handles, lead blocks, life sling, and cushions.

— In a sailboat especially, stow or secure all loose articles and gear that could fall when the boat heels or rolls. Close and latch all locker doors, and see that removable fiddles (sea rails for shelves) are in place.

— Remove sail covers and bend on a jib appropriate for the wind strength.

— Uncoil mainsheet and shackle on halyards.

— Tie on jib sheets and see that lead blocks are in the correct position (consult notebook if in doubt).

— Adjust the mainsail's outhaul. Leave it fairly slack if the breeze is light, but tighten it in a fresh wind.

— See that all battens are in their pockets.

— Check level of engine lube oil and fuel supply. (Ship's notebook should explain dipstick markings and note the number of hours that engine was run after the fuel tank was filled).

— Check engine coolant and transmission fluid.

— Turn on battery main switch, and if there is a battery condition meter, check it.

— Turn on fuel valve before starting engine, and if the engine is gasoline powered, sniff for fumes in the engine room and run the bilge blower for at least five minutes. Look for evidence of leaking oil or fuel.

— Place your hand over the blower exhaust outlet to see that a good draft of air is coming through and sniff the outlet for fumes.

— Engine starting instructions should be written in the notebook. After starting, check exhaust to see that cooling water is coming out. Let engine run for a few minutes before getting underway.

— Before casting off, check to see that no lines are hanging overboard, as they could foul the prop. Remove fenders when clear of the dock.

— If you have a folding prop, be sure its blades are unfolded. When one blade fails to open fully it will cause significant vibration. The problem can usually be corrected by momentarily shifting into reverse.

CHECKLIST FOR SECURING

Securing procedures after returning to port are nearly the reverse order of getting underway procedures.

—When approaching a dock or pier to land, break out

dock lines and hang fenders. Have crew stand by, without blocking the helmsman's view, to fend off and handle lines.

—Secure dock lines or mooring pendant (these lines will be discussed in the next section).

—Don't turn off engine immediately, but let it idle for a few minutes to dissipate residual heat gradually.

—After shutting down the engine, close fuel valve, turn off battery switch, and close cooling water seacock.

—Close head sea cocks or valves.

—Slack mainsail outhaul and put on sail cover. Lash cover with a spiral winding if boat is to be left for a long period or severe weather is expected.

—If jib is hanked on, remove it from stay and fold it or stuff it in a bag with the tack up (at the top of the bag) and stow below or in a watertight cockpit locker.

—Coil all halyards and sheets. Stow all loose lines and hang the others from their cleats or hitch the coil to the standing part of the line.

—Assemble all loose gear such as winch handles, blocks, and cushions and stow below (in areas designated in the ship's notebook).

—See that gear of any value is in a stowage location that can be locked.

—Shackle halyards away from mast or tie them off with gilguys.

—Strike (remove) all flags unless you need one aloft to keep off birds.

—Cover the binnacle to keep sun off the card.

—See that ventilators are turned the right way to admit or exhaust air but keep out water. Open all sliding locker doors below and icebox lid for ventilation.

—Check the stove to see that pressure is off and valves are closed.

— Pump dry the bilge and icebox sump. Remove excess ice.

— Remove garbage and trash.

— Enter any information needed in the ship's notebook and stow in its normal location.

— Dog hatches and insert companionway slides. Lock and stow keys in a safe location.

CASTING OFF AND MAKING FAST

Small boats often can be secured temporarily to a pier with only one line, the painter or bow line. The boat should be on the leeward side of the pier so that she will be blown downwind and avoid contact with the dock wall or pilings. Larger boats should be made fast alongside the pier with several dock lines, normally consisting of a bow and stern line and two spring lines, one leading forward and the other aft as illustrated. The latter lines prevent the boat from moving ahead or back. Although the primary function of the bow and stern lines is to hold in the ends of the boat, these lines should be led well forward and aft to allow for the rise and fall of tide. A rule of thumb is that spring lines should be about equal to the boat's overall length, while bow and stern lines should be about two thirds as long.

Make fast to pilings with a clove hitch having a half hitch around the line's standing part (see Chapter 2), or a round turn around the pile and two or more half hitches on the standing part or, preferably, the backhanded hitch (illustrated in Chapter 2). If you are putting a spliced loop over the piling and there is already a loop on it, dip the line or pass your loop through the other. This permits the removal of either line without removing the other. When cleating lines, be sure to use hitches for security. Dock

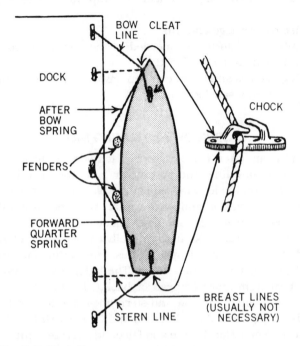

Fig. 3-2. Dock lines

lines usually should be tended from the boat, but if there
is any extra length of line lying on the pier, be sure it is
neatly coiled and placed where no one can trip over it.
When leaving a slip, dock lines that are left behind are
coiled and placed on top of the pilings or hung in such a
way that they can be reached with a boat hook when returning. If the boat is kept at a mooring, the mooring pendant's eye should be secured on its cleat by cleating the
pickup line over the eye.

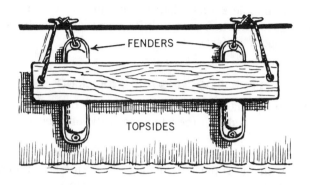

Fig. 3-3. Fender board

Be sure your boat is well fendered before leaving her made fast to a pier. Acting as a cushion to protect the topsides, a typical vinyl fender has grommets or lashing lines at each end (see illustration). If one lashing is used, it should be tied close to the rail to limit movement. When there is a projecting piling that may cause damage, the fender can be tied horizontally to the piling with both lashings. Another alternative is to use a fender board as illustrated or else a cushion board (a fender board with its own cushions). In severe weather when extra fendering is needed, old automobile tires can be used.

A most important check that should be made before leaving the boat is to see that all lines are protected from chafe. Vulnerable areas are where the lines pass through chocks or rub against rough edges of the pier. Standard chafe guards of neoprene hose with lacing lines to hold in place are satisfactory, but split tube types need heavy taping to hold them closed. Permanent mooring pendants may be protected with leather chafe kits obtainable from leading chandlers. I have found that automobile seatbelts make good antichafe material. Be sure that your chocks have smooth surfaces.

TIPS FOR DOCKING AND UNDOCKING

—When leaving a dock under sail, always hoist sail with the boat headed into the wind. Hoist the aftermost sails first.

—When shoving off, push the boat straight back (downwind) with the rudder amidships, then turn the rudder after the boat is well clear of the dock (steering will be discussed in the next chapter).

—To assist turning the boat, especially when there is no way, back the jib or hold it over on the windward side, opposite to the direction you want the boat to turn.

—Be sure that no sheets or other lines can snag on dock cleats or pilings when getting underway.

—If it is necessary to land under sail, always do so into the wind so that the sails will flap and lose their drive.

—Practice shooting (heading up into the wind) to see how much way your boat will carry. Normally, the heavier the boat, the farther she will carry, but she will shoot less far in fresh winds than in light airs.

—It is best to land at the end of a pier if possible so that the boat may be turned away at the last moment if she is moving too fast.

—If landing in the middle of the pier, be sure to approach at low speed with just enough way on to utilize the rudder. It is best to err on the slow side and have a crew member standing on the bow with a lightweight, coiled heaving line to throw to someone on the pier.

—To heave a line, coil it and hold about half the coils in each hand. Throw one half with an underhand toss, then immediately release the other half so that it can follow. Effective heaving takes a bit of practice.

— Approach a pier or mooring on a close reach (points of sailing will be explained in the next chapter) with the sails luffing slightly. Then, if more speed is needed, the sails can be trimmed in slightly, but if less speed is desired, the sheets can be slacked. When shooting, speed can be controlled somewhat by how hard the helm is turned. Easy turning does little to reduce speed, while quickly jamming the rudder hard over can slow the boat dramatically.

— On many well-balanced boats with large mainsails the landing or mooring pickup can be baldheaded (with the jib lowered), but if a jib is carried it should be a small one that is high cut (with a high foot) to allow good visibility and easy handling.

— Speed can be slowed at the last minute or after the mooring float has been grabbed by backing the mainsail or pushing the main boom forward while the boat is headed into the wind.

— Be sure to consider the current. In the unusual circumstance of a strong current against the wind, the landing or pickup might have to be made downwind under drastically reduced sail, which would be dropped at the last moment.

— In some cases, when it is necessary to dock downwind, the boat can be luffed up just to windward of the pier to lower sail, and then she can drift down on the pier, or drop an anchor and pay out the anchor line until the dock can be reached.

— Docking or picking up a mooring under power is much easier, as the engine can be reversed at the last moment to reduce speed. However, don't approach any faster than necessary for good rudder control, as the engine could possibly stall when put into reverse. This has happened

with embarrassing and sometimes disastrous consequences.

— In a gentle wind it is easier to land on the windward
side of a pier, but be sure the pier and boat are well fendered. Leaving from the windward side is more difficult,
as the boat will be blown against the pier. Avoid landing
on the windward side in a strong wind or current that
forcefully sets you against pilings or a dock wall.

— If landing on the windward side of a pier, try to be at the
end of the dock where you will not be blocked by another
boat.

— To leave from the windward side, use a bow spring line
leading aft to the pier. By going ahead on the line the stern
will be sprung outward away from the dock; then, of
course, the line is cast off and the boat quickly backed
away. During this maneuver, the bow will be pressed hard
against the pier, so be sure it is protected with a fender.

— When landing on the leeward side of a pier in a fresh
wind, an amidships spring line leading aft will bring you
alongside when going forward. An amidships spring line
leading forward will bring you in when the engine is reversed.

— It is often best to have the bow facing outward when
leaving, and this may require a turn between two parallel
piers when landing. Remember the prop's wheel effect,
which means that (when going ahead) a turn to port will
be tighter than a turn to starboard with the normal
righthand prop.

— If it is necessary to "back and fill" (alternately backing
and going ahead) to turn within a tight space, a turn to
starboard often is easier, because the righthand prop may
strongly walk the stern to port when reversed.

— Bear in mind that most boats will back into the wind as
the bow is blown off. Compensate for this by casting off

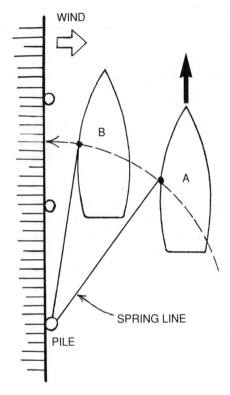

Fig. 3-4. Landing on an aft leading amidships spring line

the stern line first when backing away from the lee side of a pier and by using the rudder when steerageway is gained.

—It is considerably easier to back some boats than others. For example, boats in reverse that can throw prop wash against their rudders are easier to back. A difficult backer may need warping assistance when backing into a narrow slip when there is a beam wind.

— One method of warping into a slip is to approach the slip at right angles to it. Power up to the far outer piling and grab the line on it. Keep going ahead slowly until the stern reaches the opposite outer piling directly across the slip. Grab the line on that piling and lead it to the quarter (corner of the stern) opposite the quarter nearest the piling. With ample crew fending off and tending these lines, the boat can be swung around so that her stern enters the slip, and then she can be worked into her berth.

— A Mediterranean moor, berthing stern-to after dropping an anchor from the bow, can be a difficult maneuver in a narrow space between moored boats when there is a fresh beam wind. This procedure will be discussed in Chapter 9, which deals with anchoring and mooring.

Further docking details may be found in the Cornell Boaters Library book called *Dockmanship* by David Owen Bell.

4. Under Sail, Engine, and Oars

To a master hand she responds like a living creature.

                        —Rex Clements

No matter what the form of propulsion, a competent sailor must have full control of the vessel. Even if not a master hand, he or she can at least aspire to obtaining the best possible response. Requisites are thoroughly understanding the propulsive system and skillful helmsmanship.

BASIC STEERING

With the exception of small rowboats and most outboard motorboats, most vessels are turned with rudders, which usually are controlled with steering wheels, tillers (levers attached to rudder heads), or occasionally whip-staffs (vertical tillers). In former times, whip-staffs were most often pushed from side to side, but nowadays they normally are positioned at the sides of open boats and are pushed forward or aft to steer. Wheels steer vessels in the direction they are turned (like an automobile), but tillers work the opposite way. Moving ahead, the boat turns away from the direction the tiller is pushed (or pulled).

Common steering commands are "up helm" or "down helm." The latter expression means to push or pull the

tiller down to leeward, which turns the rudder to windward and causes the boat to turn into the wind, while "up
helm" means that the tiller should be pushed or pulled up
to windward, turning the rudder and boat away from the
wind. With a wheel these expressions can be confusing;
thus, the clearer command for wheel steering is "right
rudder" or "left rudder."

Wheel steering provides greater power but a slower response than steering by tiller. Tillers are normally preferable on small boats because of their simplicity and
advantage in quick response. On a large boat, however,
when steering requires considerable force in heavy
weather, a wheel is needed. There can be no hard and fast
rule for the smallest size of boat requiring a wheel; that
size might be somewhere between 25 and 40 feet for a
sailboat, depending on her design. Some obvious design
characteristics that affect steering are length of the keel,
shape of the hull, rig balance (see Chapter 2), and the
rudder design. Not only does the size and location of the
rudder have an effect, but also important is whether or
not the rudder is balanced, with part of the blade projecting forward of its turning axis so that water force can
assist with the turning.

A tiller should be as long as possible for leverage, but
not so long as to create flexibility or block the cockpit. Do
not tolerate any looseness or play. Use shims, tighten
nuts, or replace worn rudder head fittings to avoid excessive play, which can be harmful to good helmsmanship.
The racing sailor often uses a tiller extension, a stick attached to the end of the tiller with a universal joint to
allow the helmsman to hike out (sit far to windward) or to
sit far to leeward in light airs.

The modern steering wheel has an outside rim covering the spokes to prevent lines from fouling them and so

that the helmsman, when stationed far to one side, can continually reach the wheel. A beamy sailboat needs a large diameter wheel so that the helmsman can steer while sitting far to windward or leeward where there is often the best visibility. Gear ratio is a compromise between easy steering and quick response. A noted English authority, Captain J. H. Illingworth, has suggested that the wheel of a small yacht should turn three quarters of a rotation to move the rudder from amidships to hard over (as far as it will go). However, some sailors might prefer greater power (but slightly slower response) of a full rotation or somewhat more to produce the same rudder movement. Freedom of wheel movement is particularly important for a sailboat so that the helmsman can "feel" the vessel's response. American sailing authority Rod Stephens, Jr., has suggested a freedom of movement needing only a 1 pound weight 1 foot from the hub to move the wheel. The king spoke (upper vertical spoke when the rudder is amidships) should be marked with tape or a winding of twine that can be seen from a distance and can be felt in the dark.

SAILING

The basics of sailing should be understood by all boaters, even powerboat skippers, enabling them to anticipate the maneuvers of any sailboat they might meet in open waters and particularly in restricted areas.

The first requisite for a beginning sailor is to learn wind direction. This may be told by feel (feeling the breeze on your hands, face, and neck); watching the movement of such things as flags, smoke, or ripples on the water; noticing how vessels lie at anchor (when there is little or no current); and especially glancing frequently at wind indicators. Every sailboat should carry telltales (see Chapter 2) on its shrouds as well as on the sails and, most importantly, a wind indicating device at the masthead. The most helpful indicator is one with reference arms such as the well-known Windex. These arms are bent or otherwise set to correspond with the boat's optimal close hauled course in moderate conditions (with fairly smooth waters and moderate wind). In simple language, a close hauled course is the one closest to the wind a boat can sail without her sails beginning to luff or flap when they are trimmed in (pulled in almost as much as possible with their sheets).

Apparent Wind

Wind indicators do not show the true wind. They show the apparent wind, or what the sailor on a moving boat actually feels. When any vehicle moves ahead it creates its own breeze which becomes stronger as the speed increases (stick your hand out of a moving car's window on a calm day and feel the breeze). Thus, the apparent wind is the combination of the true wind (felt on an anchored boat) and the wind caused by boat speed. Velocity as well as direction of the apparent wind varies as the boat changes course. The apparent wind is always forward of the true wind on any heading except one that is exactly downwind. Angular differences between the two winds increase as the boat bears away from close hauled until she is about broadside to the true wind. Thereafter, as she continues to bear away, the angles decrease and there is no angular difference when the wind is dead aft. Velocity of the apparent wind is greatest when close hauled, and it progressively weakens as the boat bears away. When the wind is dead astern, the entire speed of the boat is subtracted from the true wind velocity, and of course, she

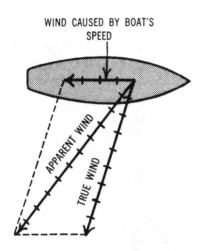

WIND CAUSED BY BOAT'S
SPEED

APPARENT WIND

TRUE WIND

Fig. 4-1. Apparent wind vector. If true wind is 9 MPH and boat speed is 4 MPH, then apparent wind is 11 MPH.

feels much less wind. Exact direction and speed of the apparent wind can be found with a simple vector diagram that shows the apparent wind as the resultant of true wind and boat speed, but this figuring is seldom necessary. The sailor can simply feel the velocity and see the direction on the wind indicator.

Points of Sailing

The three basic points of sailing are beating (sailing as close as possible to the wind with the sails sheeted in), reaching (with the wind on the boat's side and the sails sheeted more or less halfway out), and running (with the wind astern and the sails almost all the way out). However, these basic points can be further refined with addi-

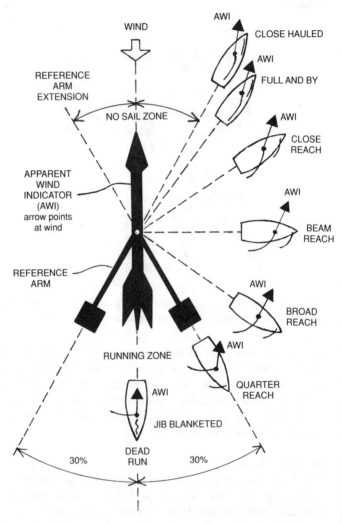

Fig. 4-2. Points of sailing with respect to apparent wind.
Boom is about 90 degrees to apparent wind in running zone
but about 30 degrees or less on other points of sailing.

tional points that are shown in the accompanying diagram. Unlike most diagrams of this kind, the points of sailing illustrated here are shown with the apparent wind (as well as the true wind) so that the sailor can determine the points with respect to the wind indicator and its reference arms. Only the port tack courses (with the mainsail on the starboard side) are shown, but obviously there are equivalent starboard tack courses (with mainsail to port) on the left-hand side of the diagram.

Most boats designed primarily for sailing (rather than for dual forms of propulsion) should be able to "sail square," that is to say, they should be able to sail sufficiently close to the wind that one close hauled tack will be at right angles to the other. Beating courses for such boats will probably vary between the close hauled and full-and-by courses shown in the diagram. Notice that the apparent wind angle for the close hauled course is shown at about 30 degrees from the direction of the true wind. Although some racing boats can sail a bit closer to the wind, 30 degrees is a good round figure for a smart sailor in a moderate breeze with smooth water, and this is about the proper angle at which the indicator's reference arms should be set. In light airs and choppy seas, the full-and-by course with slightly eased sheets normally produces the greatest VMG (speed made good) to windward.

Reaching points of sailing are divided into close, beam, broad, and quarter reaching. The former is usually the fast point of sailing in light airs, but beam reaching is generally faster in fresh winds. Sheets are eased the farther the boat bears away from the wind, but fast boat speed requires slightly closer trim as the apparent wind draws farther ahead. When beating and reaching the wind flows across the sails from luff to leech and creates a low pressure suction pull on the lee side of the sails.

As the boat bears away from the quarter reach, the sails begin to stall, i.e., the wind stops flowing across the sails from luff to leech, and the boat is propelled primarily by the wind's push rather than its pull. She is then in the running zone, which means that when the helmsman looks at the wind indicator, the arrow head of its pointer will be somewhere between the reference arms (closer to the left arm when on the port tack, as in the diagram). A running sloop would have her jib at least partially blanketed (shielded from the wind) by the mainsail. On a dead run, with the wind directly aft, the jib can be winged out (set with or without a pole on the side of the boat opposite the mainsail). Running in this manner, a boat is said to be sailing wing-and-wing.

If the port tack boat continues turning to starboard, she'll soon jibe onto the starboard tack (with her mainsail on the port side). This downwind turning maneuver causes the sails to swing across the boat suddenly, and the crew must be wary of being hit by the boom. Changing tacks by turning into the wind (with the wind on the bow) is called tacking or coming about. During this maneuver the sails do not swing across suddenly, but they luff and then flap as the boat moves through the eye of the wind.

Sailing Tips

—As noted in Chapter 3, when hoisting or lowering the mainsail, head up into the wind to keep the sail from fouling the rigging.
—Hoist the aftermost sails first to keep the bow from blowing off. Periodically glance aloft to see that all is clear while hoisting.
—Watch the water to windward for rippling and darkening wind streaks or patches to detect puffs.

—In light airs sail toward wind patches. Don't wait for them to come to you, as the wind often fills in or moves toward you very slowly.

—To control excessive heeling in fresh winds, slack sheets and luff up (head up into the wind) except when you are sailing considerably lower than a beam reach when you should bear off to almost a dead run.

—In light airs ease sheets and adjust sails for deep draft (as explained in Sail Tips, Chapter 2).

—In fresher winds flatten the sails and decrease their draft.

—When beating and reaching keep your sails on the verge of luffing. This can be done by watching the luff telltales described earlier, or by easing the sheet or heading up until the sail just begins to luff.

—The challenge when beating is to sail the boat as close to the wind as possible without a significant reduction in speed. A good helmsman develops a feel for when the boat is sailing her best, and continually prods the wind to see if the boat can't point higher (head up) without slowing down. Pinching (sailing slightly too high) not only slows the boat, but it also causes excessive leeway (side slipping).

—Use most of your senses when beating: Feel the wind, helm, and angle of heel; watch the sails, water, compass, speedometer, and telltales; listen for shaking of sails and changes in the sound of the bow wave.

—One aid to windward sailing that is seldom mentioned in sailing manuals is reading the sag of the jibstay. When the stay is straight there is little or no load on the jib, and the helmsman should bear off a bit; but when there is at least a little sag, the jib is loaded and probably pulling with efficiency. Point as high as possible while keeping some sag in the stay.

— Give plenty of warning to crew and passengers before coming about or jibing. It is customary to prepare for tacking with the command "ready about" followed by "hard-a-lee" when the tiller is actually turned to leeward (or wheel turned to windward). With jibing, the usual commands are "stand by to jibe" followed by "jibe-ho."

— When tacking do not release the jib sheet until nearly head-to-wind, as a sudden premature release may kill the boat's headway.

— Before tacking be sure the boat has ample speed to answer her helm. When coming about push the helm slowly but firmly. A sudden shift of the rudder may kill headway and cause the boat to get in stays (also called irons), i.e., come to a stop and be unable to fall off on either tack.

— If the boat is in stays, wait for her to gain sternway and then reverse the rudder (the stern will follow the rudder). Back the jib by sheeting it to the side away from the direction you want to go (pull it to port if you want to be on the port tack and vice versa for the starboard tack).

— In beating to a windward mark or other upwind destination, your last tack theoretically should be on the lay line (the most leeward close hauled course the boat can sail without tacking). If you are not racing, however, you might want to slightly overstand (sail well beyond the lay line) to assure fetching in the event of a wind shift. Overstanding, some sailors say, is like putting some money in the bank.

— To determine when you are on the lay line, wait until the windward mark bears abeam (a sighting at right angles to the boat's centerline). If the boat can sail square (considering leeway), and there is no current, she should be able to fetch or lay the mark on the opposite tack. A beam bearing can be determined with the compass (see

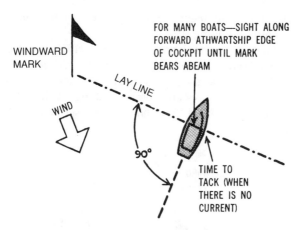

Fig. 4-3. Fetching a mark by tacking on the lay line

Chapter 6) or simply by sighting along the forward edge of the cockpit or after edge of the cabin trunk.

— When beating in shifty winds, tack on significant head-ers (unfavorable shifts).

— To increase your chances of reaching a windward mark in the quickest time, take the tack first that allows you to head closer to your destination.

— In fresh winds don't sail on a dead run or by-the-lee (a heading slightly further than a dead run toward the side of the boat the mainsail is on) unless, perhaps, you rig a preventer (a line attached to the boom leading forward) to hold the boom steady and prevent an accidental jibe.

— If running wing-and-wing in light to moderate winds, you can wing out the jib without using a pole by sailing dead downwind or slightly by-the-lee, but do so only if a jibing preventer is rigged.

—The easiest way to sail wing-and-wing without a pole is to jibe the main and leave the jib alone (rather than leaving the main and jibing the jib).

—Except perhaps in fresh winds, the most efficient way of sailing most boats to a leeward mark is by tacking downwind (sailing on one tack on a broad or quarter reach, then jibing to the equivalent point of sailing on the other tack). Take the tack first that allows the closer heading to the mark.

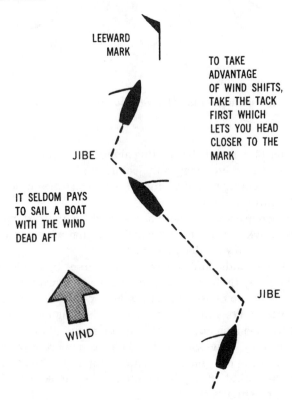

Fig. 4-4. Tacking downwind

—When running in winds of constantly varying velocity, slightly bear off (heading away from the wind) in puffs and slightly luff up (heading closer to the wind) in the lulls. Heading up causes the sails to draw more effectively and increases the apparent wind, while heading off in the puffs allows you to work your way downwind.

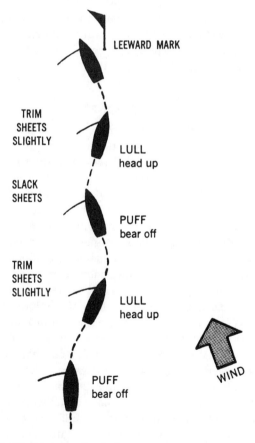

Fig. 4-5. Working downwind

—When jibing, shorten sheet (haul in the mainsheet) so that the boom cannot slam across nor the sheet foul. Do not suddenly luff up immediately after jibing, but quickly slack the mainsheet.

—To change tacks in heavy weather, consider coming about rather than jibing.

—If you are not racing, you can save labor by luffing up to trim sails and by running off to lower or change jibs. With the wind aft, the apparent wind will be less, motion will be easier, spray will be reduced, and the forward sail will be blanketed by the mainsail.

UNDER POWER

How boats handle and maneuver under power depends on such factors as hull type and design, engines, propellers, and rudders. Some examples regarding hull types and design are: high freeboard powerboats with lofty superstructures and shallow draft are greatly affected by wind force; low freeboard boats with deep draft are more affected by current; windage of rigging and spars is a major consideration for sailboats under power; boats with outboard motors or inboard motors with outboard drives, inboard-outdrives (I/Os), have maneuvering advantages in that their propellers are turned to steer; boats whose bottoms are flat, or with shallow V-sections, or with warped V-sections (Vee'd forward and flat aft) are usually quick to plane but subject to pounding in choppy seas; deep V boats with constant deadrise (see Chapter 1) that handle well in choppy seas need extra power to plane; round bottom boats tend to roll, but pounding is minimized and rolling is relatively slow; boats with long keels or skegs tend to have directional stability at some cost in responsive steering; powerboats with flattish bottoms and small skegs will skid on sharp turns; high speed planing hulls are often difficult to steer at low speeds, etc.

Engines and propellers affect boat performance and handling according to their size, type, and number. For example, twin engine/twin screw boats are much easier to maneuver at low speeds, and props rotate in opposite directions to cancel walking of the stern by wheel effect (Chapter 3). Single screw boats with their deeper propellers requiring protection from a keel or long skeg tend to track better at low speeds, but they are more difficult to maneuver. Displacement craft respond most effectively to large diameter, multi-blade propellers turning at relatively slow revolutions, whereas high speed boats normally need smaller, fast-turning props. An exception to this rule is for sailboats with auxiliary power that use small two bladed props (often with direct drive) in order to minimize drag under sail.

Many boats are overpowered, i.e., they have engines larger than necessary. This is certainly true for inboard and outboard speedboats, and it is even true for many auxiliaries. A rough rule-of-thumb formula used to determine the horsepower of a displacement sailboat's engine is H.P. = $2(R \times V \times .003)$, where R is resistance and V (hull speed in knots) is 1.34 times the square root of the waterline length (see Chapter 1). Resistance can be figured at 40 pounds (for the average boat) times displacement in short tons (1 ton = 2,000 lbs.). This is minimal horsepower, but one can see, if applying the formula to many boats, that most with inboard engines are overpowered. On the other hand, an outboard auxiliary should be powerful enough to drive the boat through strong head winds and choppy seas and be able to cruise effectively at part throttle.

Rudders were briefly discussed in Chapter 1. The important thing to remember for maneuvering ability under power is that the propeller can direct a flow of water against the rudder. On most boats this is no problem since the prop is directly forward of the rudder, but obviously the flow goes forward in reverse. High speed boats usually have tiny rudders that are effective at planing speeds but ineffective at low speeds. Always keep enough speed for steerageway. Although rudderless boats with outboard drives are highly maneuverable when under power, they are difficult to control when coasting after power has been cut. It is always prudent to learn the individual handling and maneuvering characteristics of your own boat by practicing at first in fair weather, and, if possible, in uncongested areas.

Fueling

Nothing is more important than developing good fueling habits. This is especially true where gasoline is concerned, since gas fumes have the explosive potential of dynamite, and being heavier than air, they can easily sink into a boat's bilge and possibly be ignited by a spark. With diesel fuel there is little risk of explosion, but spilled fuel can create a fire hazard, and dirt or water in the fuel can easily stop a diesel engine. Prudent fueling practice is set forth in the following rules:

— Take on fuel in the daylight and with the boat properly secured and preferably headed into the wind.
— Before fueling with gasoline, close all hatches or portholes through which fumes might enter the cabin or bilge.
— See that the fuel tank vent is open and unclogged.
— Turn off stove and don't smoke or strike matches.
— Keep nozzle of hoze from gas pump in contact with fill pipe to avoid sparks from static electricity. Be sure the pipe and tank are grounded.
— Fill the tank slowly and be careful not to overflow.

—Wipe up any spills and let the boat air out. Sniff for fumes before starting engine, and, as described in Chapter 3, run the bilge blower for at least five minutes before starting engine.

—When the fill pipe is in the bottom of the cockpit, fan out the cockpit after fueling on a calm day. This is especially important if the scuppers are submerged.

—If you have a small outboard with integral fuel tank, don't fill the tank while the engine is hot.

—When the engine is a diesel, be sure to get clean fuel, and use a funnel that has a fine screen through which the fuel must pass.

Powering Tips

—An outboard motorboat with a cutaway transom (for the sake of accomodating a short shaft engine) needs a high motor well just forward of the transom cutout. This prevents waves from sloshing over the stern and possibly swamping the boat when there is crew weight aft and the stern faces the wind.

—On high freeboard boats with stern-mounted outboards use a long shaft engine to assure the prop will remain submerged in a seaway.

—An outboard's cavitation plate, which helps prevent aeration of the prop, should be kept about three inches below the water.

—A skeg that is too close to the prop (perhaps closer than nine inches) may cause significant cavitation, particularly if the skeg end is not faired.

—Carry ample fuel (see Chapter 1 for "1/3 rule"). Reduce RPMs by one third to reduce fuel consumption by about one half.

—Be sure the engine is not in gear when it is started. Some of the older outboards can be started in gear with possible adverse consequences (such as ramming the dock or causing a crew member to lose balance).

— Clean your prop periodically, as barnacles on the blades can have a disastrous effect on performance.

— If you have a folding prop be sure both blades are fully open when starting the engine, otherwise there may be annoying and possibly damaging vibration. As covered in Chapter 3, the blades usually can be opened by momentarily shifting into reverse.

— Don't put a load on the engine until it has at least partially warmed up.

— In a small boat see that crew and passengers are positioned to give the boat proper trim, normally with the bow slightly elevated and without being listed (heeled).

— High speed boats, especially those with deep V sections aft need trim tabs (sometimes called stern flaps). These are most often hydraulically operated and controlled at the helm to trim the hull effectively and hold down the bow at high speeds.

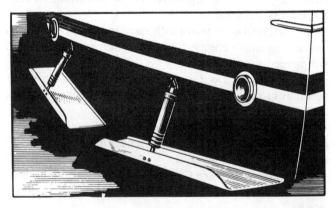

Fig. 4-6. Hydraulic trim tabs. Courtesy of Bennette Marine

—The normal trim tab adjustment when accelerating from slow speed is: To keep the bow down when starting to climb onto a plane, trim the bow slightly up when on the plane, then trim it slightly down at top speed.

—Never allow the bow to rise up too high, as this can cause pounding and porpoising (when the boat repeatedly leaps out of water), increase windage, obstruct visibility, and adversely affect the shaft angle (a shaft parallel to the water surface maximizes thrust).

—On the other hand, keep the bow up in following seas or other conditions when there is danger of the bow burying ("stuffing," in the modern vernacular). Burying the bow at high speeds can throw crew forward or even cause the boat to dive in extreme conditions.

—Small outboard boats can simulate the effect of trim tabs by tilting the outboard, trimming in (raking aft) to drive the stern up, and trimming out (raking forward) to drive the stern down.

—Be aware of a boat's pivot point (the point on which she rotates when the helm is turned). This point is usually well forward of amidships on a powerboat, and this means that the stern will swing away from the direction of the turn as illustrated.

—Don't forget the wheel effect of the propeller as described earlier. This will be most pronounced after reversing the engine, when the stern will be walked to port (with a righthand prop).

—When bucking head seas under power in an auxiliary sailboat, try motorsailing (powering and sailing simultaneously) with modest sail for extra drive. You can usually head slightly higher than a close hauled course. Sail also helps to steady the boat when seas are on the beam.

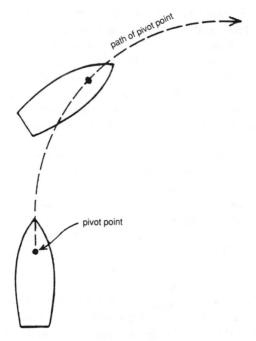

Fig. 4-7. Powerboat's pivot point

— If motorsailing when the boat is well heeled in a fresh breeze, occasionally right the boat (perhaps come about) so that the engine can obtain proper lubrication.

— If caught out in an unballasted motorboat in a sudden storm that produces short, steep, breaking seas, keep mostly end-to the seas. Normally, power slowly into the seas, or if your destination lies across wind, make a zigzag course that alternately puts the waves on the quarter and then broad on the bow (heavy weather tactics are discussed in Chapter 8.)

— Some coastal inlets are dangerous to negotiate, especially when there is heavy surf. Don't enter on an ebb tide when the current is flowing against the waves, as this can produce dangerous breakers. If you are in a fast motorboat it is usually best to ride in on the back of a wave (not on its face) at the exact speed of the wave.

— A major cause of serious motorboat accidents is operation at excessive speeds. An especially dangerous combination is an inexperienced, macho show-off behind the wheel of an overpowered runabout in a congested area. Speed should be cut in traffic and particularly when making sharp turns.

— Skippers of displacement vessels should be speed conscious because heavy boats create large wakes. Cut speed when passing close to a sailboat or any small craft. Also, remember that wakes striking a nearby shore over a period of time can cause serious erosion.

— Twin screw boats are quite easy to maneuver because they can be turned by throttling down one engine or even reversing one while the other is in forward gear. A trade-off is that twin propellers are more exposed and more difficult to protect from flotsam or grounding.

UNDER OARS

Yet another form of propulsion is oar power. With the predominance of outboard motors, it seems as though rowing has become a lost art, but a good measure of seamanship can still be judged by the way a sailor rows his or her dinghy and brings it alongside the mother vessel. Rowing is not just a method of propulsion for dinghies alone. Oars can be used to move daysailers, small powerboats, and even overnighters over short distances. The oar is almost 100 percent reliable, and it can be used for emergency secondary propulsion when the motor fails or when a sailboat is caught in a calm. I remember when a friend of mine, who is an excellent sailor and author of a book on seamanship, took his Boston Whaler to a remote island off the coast of Maine. On his way home, the engine quit and he was unable to start it. He merely shipped his oars and rowed home, thereby avoiding what could have been an awkward and possibly dangerous dilemma.

Moving a moderate size boat by oars may seem at first thought a formidable task, but in calm weather over short distances it can be done without great effort. Joshua Slocum even propelled his 16-ton *Spray* with oars when inside protected harbors. Yacht designer John Letcher has rowed his 25-foot offshore cutter *Aleutka* through a lengthy portion of the U.S. East Coast's Intracoastal Waterway. Using two 8-foot oars with oarlocks on the rail, he rows facing aft while sitting on the bridge deck just abaft the companionway. John claims that the 5,000-pound *Aleutka* is quite easy to row in smooth water, and it only takes a sixteenth of a horsepower to keep her moving at 1½ knots. The secret is to have proper rowlocks (oarlocks) and oars of sufficient length. When the boat is not so equipped, it is often possible to tow her with the dinghy. Sometimes a boat can be rowed with one oar while the helm is held over to keep her going straight.

Oarsmanship

—When boarding a small rowboat, especially a dory type (with narrow bottom) or a round bottom boat, step as close as possible to the centerline (never on the gunwale) to prevent excessive heel. Once in the boat, keep your weight as low as possible.

—See that your rowboat is properly trimmed, neither down by the bow nor down by the stern. Shift your oarlocks to the seat that provides the best trim.

— Normally, the rower faces aft, but this requires that you periodically turn your head to see where you are going. For short distances in smooth water it is often convenient to face forward and use pushing rather than pulling strokes.

— If facing aft, try to line up a nearby object astern with a distant object to form a range. This will facilitate holding a straight course.

— When rowing in the normal fashion using pulling strokes, see that there is a firm brace for your feet, as optimal power can be obtained by using your legs. When the body begins to feel the strain of a stroke, the leg muscles should be used to start pushing your feet against the brace.

— Hold your back fairly straight with head up, pivot at the hips, and lean back to accomplish a long, powerful stroke.

— Feather (twist) your oars for extra power, efficiency, and minimal windage. The blades should be about vertical when they enter the water, and then they are twisted to a near horizontal position near the end of the stroke. After leaving the water the blades are held almost horizontal until just before submersion.

— During the stroke, keep the blades near the surface and lift them no higher than necessary to clear the wave tops during the recovery (after they have been lifted clear of the water).

— When rowing against a strong wind or towing, get your oars into the water as quickly as possible, as any hesitation before a stroke will quickly stop your progress.

— Gradual turning is obviously accomplished by pulling harder on one oar than the other. Quicker turns require trailing one oar or backing one if a very tight turn is needed.

A   blade vertical

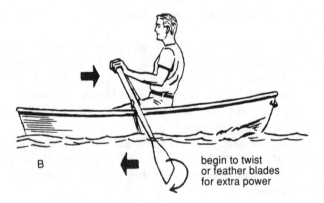

B   begin to twist
                                         or feather blades
                                         for extra power

Fig. 4-8. Feathering the oars

—When landing at a vessel or pier nearly always bring the
dinghy alongside (head-to-wind if possible) so that you
make a parallel rather than a head-on landing. Just before coming alongside bring in your inside oar and unship
its oarlock.

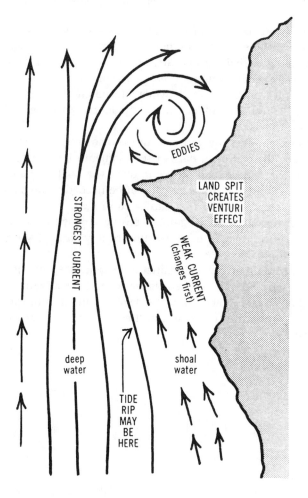

Fig. 4-9. Current strength

EDDIES

LAND SPIT
CREATES
VENTURI
EFFECT

STRONGEST CURRENT

WEAK CURRENT
(changes first)

deep
water

shoal
water

TIDE
RIP
MAY
BE
HERE

— Stow your oars on or under the seats so that they are secure and the handles do not project over the gunwales.

— Sculling is really a lost art, but a boat can be moved effectively in calm waters by extending one oar astern and moving it from side to side while alternately twisting the blade. A stern oarlock or small transom cutout is needed to hold the oar.

— When paddling by yourself, use the so-called J-stroke whereby the paddle or oar is used momentarily as a rudder at the end of each stroke to steer the boat or canoe back on course. A J-stroke will not be needed if the boat or canoe has a rudder that can be controlled.

— If rowing or paddling against a strong wind with choppy seas, try to direct your course toward a windward shore that will provide a lee.

— In paddling or rowing against a current, keep in shallow water where the current is weakest. Take advantage of eddies on the down-current side of a point or land spit. Eddies are swirls that result in limited areas of counter-current.

5. Rules of the Road

The Rules of the Road state: "If the bearing does not appreciably change, such risk (of collision) should be deemed to exist."... *Deem, hell, it damned well does exist.*
—Roger C. Taylor

As seaman/author Roger Taylor points out, some Rules of the Road sound a bit understated, although not to the degree of that oft-quoted expression attributed to the ancient Greek historian Thucydides: "A collision at sea can ruin your entire day." At any rate, knowledge of the nautical Rules of the Road is absolutely essential, and a book containing details, such as *Navigation Rules* published by the U.S. Coast Guard, should be carried on every cruising boat. In fact, this book is required on boats over 12 meters (39.4 feet) long. The governing regulations are covered under Inland Rules for U.S. inland and coastal waters, and International Rules for the high seas and waters outside of demarcation lines. These lines, described in the above mentioned book *Navigation Rules*, are shown on large scale charts. In general, with the exception of Annex V to the Inland Rules, the International and Inland Rules are very similar in both content and format.

RIGHT OF WAY—POWER

In at least one respect, basic principles involving right of way on the water are quite similar to those on land in the

United States. A boat under power keeps to the right-hand side of a channel just as an automobile keeps to the right-hand side of a road. When two vessels are converging head-to-head, each vessel turns to the right and passes port to port. There is an exception to this rule, however, for boats operating on the Great Lakes and western rivers such as the Mississippi and its tributaries, where a vessel heading down current has the right of way and may choose the manner of passing a vessel headed upstream with the initiation of whistle signals (see Inland Rule 14).

When vessels not on the Great Lakes or western rivers meet head on or nearly so, they pass on the port side of each other unless they are so far to starboard as not to be considered meeting head-on.

Although not mentioned in the Rules of the Road, the danger zone concept is a helpful way to determine who has the right of way in a converging or crossing situation. The danger zone is the sector from dead ahead to two points (22½ degrees) abaft the starboard beam (see illustration). If you are under power, another boat approaching from any direction in that sector has the right of way and you must give way, normally by turning to starboard and passing astern of the right of way boat. Notice in the diagram that the right of way boat is labeled "stand-on." This means that she must hold a steady course and constant speed.

If a boat approaches you from the port side or from astern you have the right of way. Any boat converging with you from a sector extending from abaft the danger zone to 22½ degrees abaft the port beam is considered an overtaking boat and she has the responsibility to keep clear.

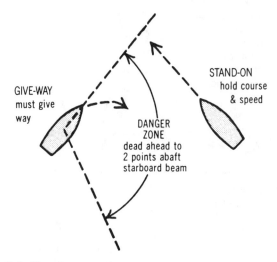

Fig. 5-1. The danger zone

RIGHT OF WAY—SAIL

The rules mentioned so far are for motorboats, including sailboats under power. Sailboats (boats under sail alone) have the right of way over motorboats except when a sailboat is overtaking a motorboat, or the latter is fishing with gear that hampers maneuverability, or the vessel under power is a large one with deep draft in a narrow channel or other waters that restrict her maneuverability. When sailing vessels converge with each other they abide by different rules:

— A starboard tack boat has the right of way over one on the port tack.
— When boats are on the same tack, the one to leeward has the right of way.

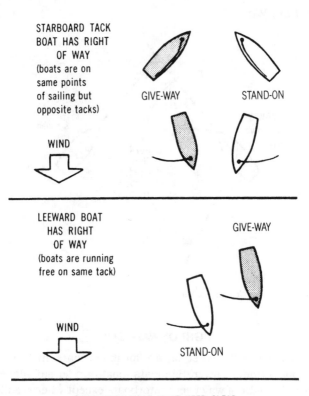

STARBOARD TACK
BOAT HAS RIGHT
OF WAY
(boats are on
same points
of sailing but
opposite tacks)

WIND

GIVE-WAY   STAND-ON

LEEWARD BOAT
HAS RIGHT
OF WAY
(boats are running
free on same tack)

WIND

GIVE-WAY

STAND-ON

OVERTAKING BOAT MUST KEEP CLEAR
EVEN IF OVERTAKEN BOAT IS UNDER POWER

GIVE-WAY   STAND-ON

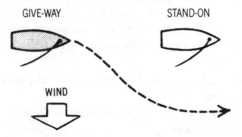

WIND

Fig. 5-2. Right of way for boats under sail

— If a port tack boat cannot determine which tack a windward boat is on, she shall keep out of the other's way.

Remember that any vessel that overtakes another must keep clear, whether under sail or not.

SOUND SIGNALS

Technically, power-driven vessels should make sound signals with a whistle (horn) when they are visible and (under Inland Rules) within half a mile of each other. However, this is not often done unless there is fairly imminent danger of a collision. At any rate, a horn should always be readily available in case it is needed to initiate or answer signals. Sound signals are similar for both Inland and International Rules except when overtaking.

Head-on or Near Head-on Meetings

— *One short blast* means "I am altering my course to starboard" under International rules or "I intend to leave you on my port side" under Inland Rules.

— *Two short blasts* mean "I am altering my course to port" (International) or "I intend to leave you on my starboard side" (Inland).

— *Three short blasts* mean "I am operating astern propulsion."

As an aid to remembering the initial rule, it may be helpful to think: *Do the right thing first* (turn right—one blast).

Overtaking

—*One short blast* under Inland Rules when an overtaking boat intends passing on the overtaken boat's starboard side.

— Two short blasts under Inland Rules when the overtaking boat intends passing on the overtaken boat's port side.

The overtaking signals under International rules are similar in concept, but one short blast is preceeded by two prolonged blasts and two short blasts are preceeded by two prolonged blasts (see Rule 34 for details).

— One prolonged, one short, one prolonged, one short blast—agreement signal sounded by boat being overtaken (International Rules). Under Inland Rules the boat being overtaken simply repeats signals initiated by the overtaking boat.

— Five short and rapid blasts (or more)—disagreement or danger. The danger signal is sounded when there is disagreement or doubt by the vessel being overtaken or by any vessel misunderstanding the intentions of another in close proximity.

Fog or Restricted Visibility (Night or Day)

— One prolonged blast sounded (at intervals of not more than two minutes) by a power-driven vessel making way.

— Two prolonged blasts in succession with about two seconds between them (same interval as above) sounded by a power-driven vessel making no way.

— One prolonged blast followed by two short blasts (same interval) sounded by a sailing vessel underway, a towing or pushing vessel, a fishing vessel (underway or anchored), a vessel restricted in her ability to maneuver (underway or anchored), or a vessel not under command.

— One prolonged blast followed by three short blasts sounded by vessel being towed (the last one if more than one being towed) immediately after the towing vessel's signal.

— *Ringing a bell rapidly for about 5 seconds* at intervals of not more than one minute for vessels at anchor. In addition, the vessel may sound in succession *one short, one prolonged, and one short blast* to warn an approaching vessel. (For full details read Rule 35).

Drawbridge

— *One prolonged blast with one short blast* following within three seconds is the usual signal for a vessel wishing to open a drawbridge. Make the signal even if the bridge is open.

LIGHTS AND SHAPES

Navigation lights are exhibited between sunset and sunrise for the obvious purpose of making a vessel visible in the dark, but these lights, especially on large vessels, can provide some additional information such as direction of travel, size, and activity. With the exception of sailboats under 7 meters (23 feet) long and boats propelled by oars, which are only required to have "ready at hand" a flashlight, all vessels operating at night need navigation lights consisting of one or more of the following:

Single all-round light (*white*) having 360 degree (32 point) visibility (can be seen from any direction). This is the only navigation lighting requirement under International Rules for a power-driven boat less than 7 meters (23 feet) having a top speed of 7 knots. It may be used with side- lights (International and Inland) on powerboats less than 12 meters (39.4 feet). A white all-round light is also used on a boat at anchor.

— Sidelights (*green*) on the starboard side, covering a visibility arc of 112½ degrees (10 points). This sector is from dead ahead to two points abaft the starboard beam (corresponding with the danger zone). Sidelights (*red*) on the port side covering a similar arc (see illustration). Except for the boats under 7 meters mentioned above, sidelights are required on all vessels underway at night.

— Stern light (*white*) at the stern showing aft, covering a visibility arc of 135 degrees (12 pts.) Other than for the exceptions mentioned above, all boats under way need stern lights. They complement the sidelights by completing the circle of lighting as illustrated.

— Single masthead (steaming) light (*white*) on the mast facing forward with a visibility arc of 225 degrees (20 points) carried when a boat is under power. Rules of the Road call this a masthead light, but it is often referred to as a steaming light because it is shown only by power vessels.

— Range lights (*white*)—another masthead light abaft and higher than the steaming light required on vessels 164 feet or longer. Although not referred to as range lights in the Rules of the Road, the two masthead lights make a useful range, since the lower light is on the forward part of the vessel and the higher one is aft. As shown in the accompanying illustration, when the range lights are seen close together, the vessel is headed toward you.

— Multiple masthead lights (*white*)—one above the other in a vertical line—indicates that the vessel is towing or pushing. Three vertical masthead lights indicate that the length of tow exceeds 200 meters (656.2 ft.).

— Towing light (*yellow*) facing aft and having the same visibility arc as a sternlight—shown (in addition to multiple masthead lights) when vessel has a tow astern. When pushing or towing alongside no towing light is needed under International Rules, but two vertical towing lights are needed under Inland Rules.

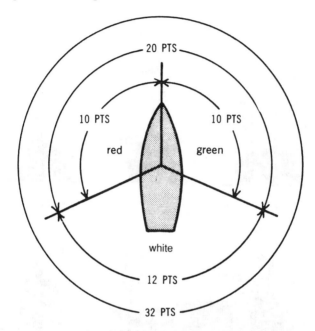

Fig. 5-3. Arcs of visibility for sidelights and stern light

— Multiple all-round lights (*white, red,* or *green*) 360 degree visibility arcs—these lights, in groups of two or three, are for vessels limited in their ability to maneuver.

Examples of lighting are shown in the following section that contains doggerel intended to assist the memory. Consult the aforementioned Coast Guard publication *Navigation Rules* for complete details.

Mnemonics for Lights

— One white light—anchored at night. (Only a single all-round light.)

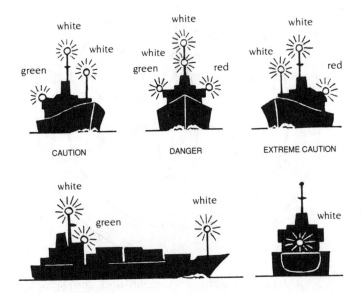

Fig. 5-4. Ship lights (note that the upper right-hand ship is in your danger zone)

—White over white—a tow is in sight. (Vertical masthead lights—pushing or towing when the towed vessel is close astern.)

—Three white lights in a row—barge is in tow. (Three vertical masthead lights when the tow exceeds 200 meters.)

—White over red—pilot boat ahead. (Vertical all-round lights.)

—Red over white—fishing tonight. (Vertical all-round lights, when fishing with gear other than trawls, which hamper maneuverability.)

—White under green—trawls are astream. (Vertical all-round lights when trawling.)

—Red over red—the head (captain) is dead. (Vertical all-round lights, when vessel is not under command or aground.)

—Red over green—sails to be seen. (Vertical all-round lights, optional lighting carried with normal sidelights and stern light by a sailboat.)

—Three reds in a line—the channel is mine. (Vertical all-round lights—vessel constrained by her draft.)

—Red, white, red—ruddy when restricted (RWR = RWR). (Vertical all-round lights shown by a vessel restricted in her ability to maneuver. Restricted lights plus two vertical red lights on obstructed side, plus two vertical greens on clear side are shown by vessel dredging or engaged in underwater operations when an obstruction exists).

—Red, white red: divers under the bay—restricted—except by day when they must show an A. (Divers on any waters show the restricted lights but during the day display a rigid code flag A.)

—Three of green—sweep it clean. (Three green all-round lights arranged in a triangle shown by a minesweeper—dangerous for another vessel to approach closer than 1,000 meters [500 on either side and 1,000 meters astern—Inland Rules].)

Shapes

Some of the messages conveyed by lights at night must be conveyed during the day with black shapes comprised of balls, cones, or cylinders. Two cones can be hung together (one above the other in close proximity) to form a diamond or an hourglass. Some commonly seen day shapes are:

—One ball, displayed by a vessel at anchor (think: ball and chain). Vessels less than 7 meters (23 feet) when anchored clear of fairways or channels are not required to show anchor lights or shapes.

— Two balls in a vertical line—vessel not under command. (Corresponds to the two red lights shown at night.)

— Three balls in a vertical line—vessel aground. (May be thought of as not under command balls with an anchor ball). Three balls forming a triangle—mine sweeping. (Corresponds to triangular lights.)

— One cone (apex down)—vessel is under sail and power. (Not required under Inland Rules when vessel is under 12 meters [39.4 ft.].)

— One cylinder—may be displayed by a vessel constrained by her draft. (Think: deep shape—deep draft.)

— One diamond (two cones with bases touching)—displayed by towing vessel less than 50 meters when tow exceeds 200 meters; by vessel being towed (towline more than 200 meters); by semisubmerged tow (one diamond aft and another forward when tow exceeds 200 meters).

— One hourglass (two cones with points touching)—vessel trawling or fishing. (When vessel is under 20 meters [65.6 ft.] a basket may be displayed.) A cone with point up is displayed in the direction of fishing gear if the gear is more than 150 meters long. (Think: fishing takes time— an hourglass.)

— Ball over diamond over ball—vessel restricted in maneuverability (corresponds to restricted lights), plus anchor ball if anchored. Restricted shapes plus two vertical balls on obstructed side and two vertical diamonds on clear side shown by vessel engaged in dredging or underwater operations when an obstruction exists.

— Divers flag (red with diagonal white stripe)—shown when diver is not connected to boat. Rigid A flag is used when diving restricts vessel's ability to maneuver.

COLLISION AVOIDANCE

Most collisions occur as a result of failure to keep a look-out. This is often due to inattention but sometimes due to blocked or partially blocked vision as a result of obstructions such as low cut sails, spray dodgers, high bows, lofty cabin trunks or superstructure, gear such as fenders on the pulpit, or reflections on windshields. To improve the helmsman's vision take the following measures:

— When luff length permits, raise the jib's foot with a tack pendant (see Chapter 2).

— Elevate the helmsman with a seat or cushions so that he or she can see ahead over the cabin trunk, high bow, or other obstruction.

— Keep crew or passengers out of the helmsman's field of vision.

— Use trim tabs to hold the bow down.

— Lower hatch covers and dodgers in congested waters.

— Clear away gear, especially at the bow, that obstructs the view.

— Minimize windshield reflections with paint, canvas covers, or other means. The helmsman should shift position frequently and/or shift head position to minimize disturbing reflections.

When visual obstructions cannot be removed, there should be a special lookout stationed where the view is clear. Above all, it is vital to stay alert and be continually watchful for other vessels that are approaching from any direction.

If another vessel some distance away is headed toward you and you are uncertain as to whether or not you are on a collision course, take a series of bearings on the approaching vessel. When the bearings definitely change

Fig. 5-5. Tack pendant

you will miss, but if they remain constant you will surely collide. A bearing is the horizontal direction of an object from an observer expressed as an angle. This angle may be measured with various devices that will be described in Chapter 6, but a quick and crude means of sighting an approaching vessel and determining a change in bearing is to sight with your hand over the top of the steering compass. If you can hold your head and course steady, you can even sight the approaching boat by lining it up with a fixed object on your boat such as a stanchion (see diagram). When there is land behind the approaching boat you can line up the boat with a tree, building, or other object on shore to see if she is "making shore" (moving along the land). Failure to make shore when holding a steady course means that the bearing is steady and you are apt to experience an "encounter of the 'thud kind'."

Be sure your bearings change drastically when you are on a collision course. If you have the right of way, hold a steady course and speed (the approaching boat must make the bearings change), but when very close (in extremis), there being imminent danger of collision, the right of way boat can (and should) alter course (see Rule 2 b, known as The General Prudential Rule). Have your horn ready in case the helmsman of the other boat is inattentive or doesn't see you. A last minute emergency turn should usually be to the right.

A basic principle of collision avoidance is to make your move early. When the approaching boat is fairly far away make an obvious turn that clearly shows your intention. Don't wait until the last moment, when close aboard, to change course.

At night try not to head directly for a distant approaching vessel, as any yawing (inadvertent turning from side

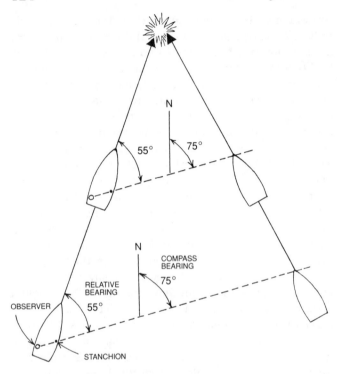

Fig. 5-6. The danger of a constant bearing

to side) you do, as a result of following seas, could confuse her lookout who might see your green light one moment and then your red light the next or vice versa. Show her one sidelight only.

A particular hazard to small craft is ships which cannot easily maneuver or slow down. A fact to bear in mind when close to a large ship is that it takes from four to six minutes for her to stop when her engines are in reverse. If you are the skipper of a small boat stay as far as possible away from large vessels, especially at night. Keep out of ship channels when possible, and never try to cross the bow of a ship unless she is far away. It is easy to underestimate the speed of an approaching ship. In most waters she will be traveling at or faster than a speed that allows best maneuverability, between 10 and 13 knots.

The small navigation lights on small craft are difficult to see from a distance, and on a sailboat they are often blocked by sails. Aside from the red over green sailboat lighting option mentioned previously, there is a helpful option for sailboats under 20 meters (65.6 feet), which allows a single masthead lantern that combines the side-lights and stern light (Rule 25). Having the navigation lights at the very top of the mast assures that they won't be blocked by sails, and the lofty location makes them more visible from the bridge of a ship. When close to a large vessel, periodically shine a bright light on your sails.

A radar reflector hung high in the rigging increases your visibility to vessels using radar, but don't assume that radar is always being used and continually monitored. In ambiguous crossing or passing situations vessels can be contacted by radio on VHF channels 13 or 16.

COURTESY AND COMMON SENSE

Legalities aside, one ingredient of seamanship is consideration for others. The following rules of courtesy and common sense seem obvious, but they are often violated.

—Avoid boats that are racing or obviously engaged in other forms of competition such as predicted log runs. Racing sailboats usually carry racing flags on their backstays.

—Watch your wake. Don't come close to small craft, boats at anchor, or any vessel under sail when you are under power and creating large stern waves. When possible, pass astern of sailboats.

—Slow down when in constricted or congested waters whether or not speed limits are posted.

—A large sailboat passing a smaller one should try to pass to leeward to avoid blanketing the smaller boat (stealing her wind).

—Whenever possible the skipper of a sailboat should avoid tacking through a narrow channel where there are large vessels restricted in their ability to maneuver (see Rule 9).

—Never anchor in a narrow channel. Fishermen often do.

—Windsurfers are subject to the same Rules of the Road as any vessel.

—Some sport fishermen who are trolling often think they have the right of way over sailboats, but this is not true (see Rule 3 d). They should maneuver to keep well clear of boats under sail and even those under power that could get fishing lines wrapped around their propellers.

—Even if they have the right of way, however, sailboat skippers should stay as far away as possible from fishermen. Sailors should realize that many powerboat skippers don't entirely understand a sailboat's maneuvering limitations. Try to delay tacking until a powerboat has passed by.

—Powerboat skippers should learn the basic principles of sailing. They should at least understand that a sailboat cannot sail into the wind, that the average sailboat is relatively deep in draft, and that wake waves can cause an inadvertent jibe when running dead before the wind.

—Water-skiers must be responsible not only to their tows but also to other boats in their vicinity. Waterskiing should not be done in congested areas, and there should be a lookout aside from the helmsman.

—A competent lookout on any boat should periodically check every direction around a 360-degree circle.

6. Piloting in a Nutshell

*In all the devious tracings the course of a sailing
ship leaves upon the white paper of a chart she is always aiming for that one little spot—maybe a small
island in the ocean, a single headland upon the long
coast of a continent, a light-house on a bluff, or simply the peaked form of a mountain like an ant heap
afloat upon the waters. But if you have sighted it on
the expected bearing, then the landfall is good.*
— Joseph Conrad

Whether making a landfall from the open sea or piloting
along a coast or in inland waters, successful navigation
provides a definite feeling of accomplishment and satis-
faction. Conversely, unsuccessful navigation, especially
when it results in a grounding, can cause at least considerable aggravation, or worse.

Piloting can be defined as coastal or inland navigation
when a vessel's position is obtained from sound signals,
soundings, and visual objects such as landmarks, buoys,
and other navigation aids. Dead reckoning (DR), the practice of finding your position by timing your run over a
known course, will also be included under the discus-
sion of piloting. Celestial navigation (deriving one's position from the sun, stars, and other celestial bodies) is
covered in a number of books, including the Cornell
Boaters Library book *How to Navigate Today* by Leonard
Gray.

ESSENTIAL TOOLS

Any boat that ventures away from familiar waters needs the following basic navigational equipment:

— Compass. A steering compass mounted forward of the helm in a position where it can be seen easily by the helmsman in normal steering positions and where deviation is minimal (deviation, or local magnetic error caused by ferrous metals or electrical elements, will soon be discussed). The compass has been called the single most important piece of navigational equipment aboard any boat.

— Deviation card. A card, readily accessible to the navigator and helmsman, that notes deviation errors in the steering compass. A simple form of deviation card is illustrated (more about this later).

FOR MAGNETIC COURSE		STEER	DEV.
N	000°	355°	(5E)
	045	042	(3E)
E	090	091	(1W)
	135	137	(2W)
S	180	184	(4W)
	225	228	(3W)
W	270	268	(2E)
	315	311	(4E)

Fig. 6-1. Simple deviation card

— Charts. Second only to the compass in navigational importance are the nautical maps called charts, which provide such essential information as water depth, channel markers and other navigational aids, landmarks, shoal water delineations, ranges, and much more. Charts come in many different forms and scales. *General charts* cover large areas with scales from 1:100,000 to 1:600,000; *coast charts* cover moderately large areas with scales from 1:50,000 to 1:100,000; and *harbor charts* cover small areas in greater detail with scales larger than 1:50,000. The scale ratios mean that one unit on the chart corresponds to the large number in the ratio of the same unit on the earth. Remember: *small scale = large area, large scale = small area.*

— Parallel rules or course protractor. Parallel rules are movable parallel straightedges used to shift courses or bearings on a chart. A course protractor, serving the same purpose, is usually a plastic instrument consist-

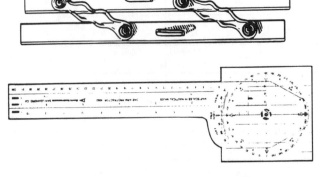

Fig. 6-2. Parallel rules and one-arm protractor (Courtesy Celestaire Navigation Instruments)

ing of a circle or arc marked in degrees and having movable arm(s).

—Dividers. An instrument with two movable arms used to measure distance from a scale on the chart.

—Drawing compass. An instrument for drawing circles on your chart.

—Binoculars. At least one binocular, preferably a 7 × 50 (7 magnifying power × 50 millimeters diameter of the front lens), which is excellent for use at night. Magnification greater than 7 power is not recommended for boats in rough waters, as the glasses are too difficult to hold steady. It is highly desirable that binoculars have a field of view of at least 400 feet at 1,000 yards away or a field angle of 7.6 degrees as illustrated (feet can be converted to degrees by dividing by 52.5).

—Bearing instruments. A bearing measures the horizontal angle between an object (buoy, for example) and the vessel's heading or magnetic north on her compass. The most common instruments for this purpose are the hand-bearing compass, bearing-taking monocular or binocular, pelorus, and sextant. More will be said about these devices soon.

—Depth-sounder or lead-line. A reliable electronic depth-sounder is much more practical than a lead-line to provide water depth, as it gives continous readings with no

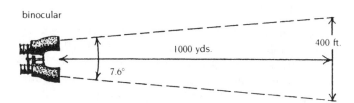

Fig. 6-3. Binocular field of view

effort and can reach considerable depths. Nevertheless, a line, preferably marked at 3-foot intervals with a weight on its end, should be carried as a backup.

— Knotmeter (speedometer) or taffrail log. To navigate by dead reckoning you need to know the speed of your boat. Experienced sailors can often judge their speed with reasonable accuracy, but an electronic knotmeter or a taffrail log with a rotator at the end of a line towed astern (to record distance) provides much greater accuracy.

— Timepiece. An ordinary watch will do for dead reckoning, but an additional stopwatch is desirable.

— Pencils and erasers (including a kneaded eraser for cleaning up charts).

— A pocket calculator, preferably solar-powered, is highly desirable.

— Electronic position finders. Any boat that travels in fog or other conditions of reduced visibility would benefit from one or more of the following instruments:

> RDF (radio direction finder).
>
> Loran (a pulsed, low-frequency radio system providing hyperbolic lines of position).
>
> Radar (radio detecting and ranging in the form of a transmitter, receiver, rotating antenna, and screen).
>
> GPS (global positioning system using radio signals from satellites).

— Publications. For distant coastal passages you should have the following publications: *Coast Pilots* (Rockville, MD: National Ocean Service), containing details of coastlines, channels, and ports; *Light Lists* (U.S. Coast Guard or Superintendent of Documents, Washington, D.C.), describing navigational aids; and *Tidal Current Tables* or charts from the National Ocean Service.

COMPASS TIPS

—Don't use a powerboat compass on a monohull sailboat. The former does not have the range of gimballing to allow for high angles of heel. Gimballing should extend through 40 degrees.

—When installing the compass be sure the lubber line (reference line or post against which the course is read) is exactly on or parallel to the vessel's fore and aft center-line. Check the alignment occasionally.

—To minimize deviation, don't mount the compass closer than 6 feet from massive ferrous objects such as the engine or 3 feet from electronic gear. Electric wires near the compass should be twisted to cancel their magnetic fields.

—As most people know, north on a magnetic compass doesn't point at the geographic North Pole but at the magnetic north pole, which is located just above Hudson Bay. The angular difference between the poles is variation. The compass roses (compass circles of degrees) printed on a chart show true and magnetic north. Working from the magnetic rose (inner circle) avoids having to correct for variation.

—Most magnetic compasses have built-in corrector magnets controlled with slot-head screws that can be turned with a nonmagnetic screwdriver. These magnets are to minimize deviation, and they are usually most effective on boats that don't heel very much. A simple means of "swinging ship" to determine deviation errors is to anchor the boat on a range (where two objects shown on the chart line up) as shown in the accompanying illustration and compare the magnetic bearings from the chart with the compass bearings as illustrated on all cardinal (N, E, S, W) headings. Half the errors should be removed with the north-south (NS) corrector magnets when the boat is

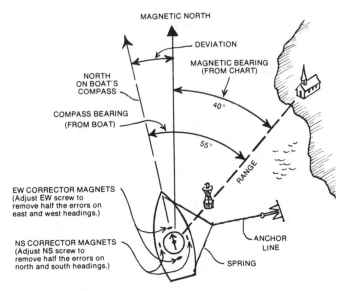

NOTE: After finding the deviation on the northerly heading, find it in a
similar way for easterly, southerly and then westerly headings.

Fig. 6-4. Correcting for compass deviation

headed north and south. Likewise, half the errors should
be removed with east-west (EW) corrector magnets when
the boat is headed east and west. The anchor and spring
line shown in the illustration suggest one method, when
weather permits, of aligning the boat with the range and
turning her to the cardinal headings. An additional stern
anchor might be needed in less than ideal conditions of
wind and current.

—If the compass bearing is greater than the magnetic
bearing from the chart, the deviation is west. Remember
the expression "compass best, error west" or "compass
least, error east".

—A simplified mnemonic to correct for deviation when steering a compass course is the phrase "can do more" with the initial letters standing for *compass, deviation, magnetic.* Then think AEC (as in Atomic Energy Commission) standing for *add east correcting* (obviously, west deviation would be subtracted). Correcting means going from compass to magnetic (for example, taking a compass course and plotting the course, corrected for deviation, on your chart). When going from magnetic to compass (for example, plotting a course on the chart and figuring a course to steer) you do the opposite: subtract east (you can use the mnemonic "east is least"). If you are confused about when you are correcting, remember that correcting begins with a C as does compass, thus correcting means going from compass to magnetic.

—If there is significant heeling error on a monohull, a professional compass adjuster should be consulted. There are two schools of thought on correcting: To remove all magnets, or to add a corrector magnet directly below the compass. An adjuster can determine what is best for your particular boat.

—Deviation corrections are more easily compensated for on some of the new electronic fluxgate compasses that use magnetometers to sense position relative to the earth's magnetic field. After initial installation, the boat need only be steered through 360 degrees for the compass to collect deviation information which is used for automatic compensation. A word of warning about fluxgate compasses, however—they cannot operate when there is electrical failure.

—Periodically check your compass for deviation by heading on known courses obtained from the chart. This is especially important after commissioning each year or loading the boat for a long cruise.

— Always keep your compass covered when not in use, as long exposure to the sun can fade the card and/or craze the plastic dome.

BEARINGS

An essential part of piloting is taking bearings. These are important not only for determining compass deviation, but especially for acquiring lines of position (LOPs) to determine your location. An LOP is a line (drawn on the chart) on which you are located. A bearing is *relative* when it measures the angle between an object and the boat's heading, and the bearing is magnetic when it measures the angle between the object and magnetic north. The principle instruments used for taking bearings have already been listed. Some brief details follow.

— Hand bearing compass. An instrument normally with a handle, compass, and sights for magnetic bearings. Accuracy depends on the accuracy of the compass and its deviation. A fluxgate handbearer has an advantage over the

Fig. 6-5. Davis handbearing compass (Courtesy Davis and Celestaire Navigation Instruments)

conventional magnetic kind in that there is no need to wait for the card to settle down, but leveling the instrument is more critical with a fluxgate. Many of the newer fluxgates have the ability to store bearings for later recall.
— Steering compass. Accurate bearings can be taken with the steering compass when it is flat and is fitted with sights. When the compass has a magnifying dome, as is the case with most modern compasses, only approximate bearings can be obtained in a crude way by sighting with a pencil or the edge of your hand held just above the dome.
— Pelorus. A dummy compass card normally oriented to the boat's centerline, that is gimballed and can be rotated, fitted with a sighting vane. It is particularly useful for taking relative bearings. At least one type has a clamp for easy mounting. A portable RDF with a rotating sight can also be used as a pelorus.
— Bearing monoculars or binoculars. Telescopic devices with built-in compasses to serve the double purpose of

Fig. 6-6. Davis pelorus (Courtesy Davis and Celestaire Navigation Instruments)

magnification and taking magnetic bearings. One type, the DataScope, incorporates a chronometer (to record time of bearings) and a range finder (to find distance from object sighted).

—Sextant. Normally used to measure the altitude of celestial bodies, the sextant can be held horizontally to obtain precise bearings. For the purpose of bearings, inexpensive plastic sextants such as the one illustrated

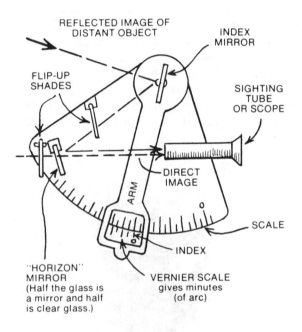

Fig. 6-7. Simple sextant. Note: *Some sextants have a micrometer screw instead of vernier scale to give minutes (1 min. equals* 1/60 *of a degree).*

can be used effectively. In using the horizontal sextant for a relative bearing, the observer (on the boat's centerline) can view a distant object (buoy, for example) through the sighting tube with the sextant's arm set at 0 degrees on the index scale, and then move the arm until the fore and aft reference point on the boat (permanent backstay or mainsail sail track, for example) is aligned with the distant object. After the object and reference point are brought together, the bearing angle is read off the index scale. The sextant is also handy for measuring angles between objects and heights of objects to obtain circles of position (soon to be explained).

Although the sextant and pelorus give relative bearings, magnetic bearings can be figured easily by noting the boat's compass heading at the times of observation and then adding or subtracting the bearings (as shown by the sextant angles in the illustrated example).

PLOTTING BASICS

The most common method of plotting (drawing on the chart) a magnetic bearing is to place parallel rulers on the chart's magnetic compass rose (inner circle), position them to correspond with the bearing angle, locate on the chart the object (buoy, for example) from which the bearing was taken, walk (move one ruler at a time without allowing slippage) the parallel rulers over to the object, and then draw the LOP.

The reverse procedure is used when laying off a course on the chart. A course line from your location to your destination or way point (a point between you and destination) is drawn on the chart, and the line is moved with parallel rules (or other instrument) to the compass rose to find out the compass course you must steer.

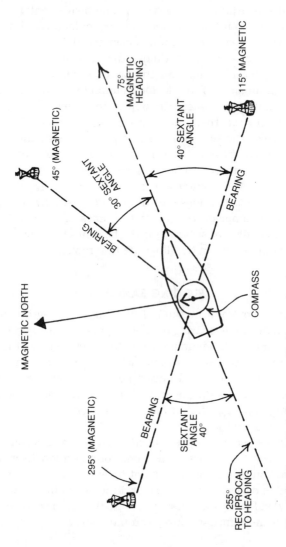

Fig. 6-8. Magnetic bearings with the sextant

MAGNETIC NORTH

45° (MAGNETIC)

115° MAGNETIC

75° MAGNETIC HEADING

40° SEXTANT ANGLE

30° SEXTANT ANGLE

BEARING

BEARING

COMPASS

295° (MAGNETIC)

BEARING

SEXTANT ANGLE 40°

255° RECIPROCAL TO HEADING

There are other instruments that serve the same purpose as parallel rulers, such as course plotters and protractors. Instructions for use are normally included when such instruments are purchased.

When plotting a course, you may want to measure the distance of the course or each leg of the course. This is especially important in fog. To measure distance, dividers are used in conjunction with a chart scale. Either measure a leg and move it to the scale or measure a unit on the scale (such as 3 miles) and move it to the course. Distance is often easily determined from lines of latitude and the scale between the lines. Keep in mind that one minute of latitude is equal to one nautical mile and sixty minutes (of arc) equals one degree (one nautical mile is 1.1516 statute miles).

LOPs, FIXES, AND DISTANCE OFF

— Two or more LOPs crossing each other provide a fix (your precise location if the LOPs are exact).

— LOPs are hardly ever exact, so a fix should be considered approximate. The closer to right angles the LOPs cross each other, the more accurate the fix should be, provided other errors (such as compass or sighting inaccuracies) are minimal.

— When three LOPs cross they normally form a triangle often called a "cocked hat" (see illustration). Assume that you are located near the middle of the triangle in open water, but in other waters, that you are on the angle nearest a shoal or obstruction to assure keeping clear.

— A circle of position (a circular LOP) is established when you can determine your distance from an object (a lighthouse, for example) or when you can measure the angle between two objects. The accompanying illustration shows

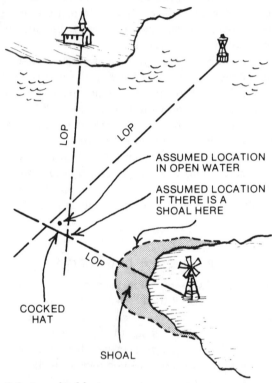

ASSUMED LOCATION
IN OPEN WATER

ASSUMED LOCATION
IF THERE IS A
SHOAL HERE

COCKED
HAT

SHOAL

Fig. 6-9. A cocked hat

a circle of position (COP) obtained by measuring the angle
between a distant water tank and church. The horizontal
angle of 75 degrees would remain the same wherever one
is located on the circle. To obtain the center of the circle
(in order to draw it with a drawing compass), draw a
straight line between the church and tank and subtract
the horizontal angle from 90 degrees. Then, as shown in

the illustration, draw from each object radius lines (RL1 and RL2) that will intersect at the circle's center. The radius lines are drawn at angles from the connecting line equal to 90 degrees minus the horizontal angle.

—A fix can be established by crossing an LOP with a circle of position obtained by measuring the angle between objects or by using the distance off as the radius of a circle. Of course, two or more COPs crossing at wide angles also can be used for a fix.

—Still another fix is the *running fix* where only one object is used to obtain two LOPs after a delay in time between bearings (see illustration). The first LOP is advanced along the course line the distance the boat has traveled, and then the first LOP is crossed with the second. The distance traveled is determined by dead reckoning, which will soon be discussed.

—*Distance off* (your distance away from a tall object of known height) can be determined with the sextant by measuring the vertical angle between a line from the observer's eye to the top of the object and a line from the eye to the sea horizon. "Distance by vertical angle" tables can be found in navigation manuals, but an approximately accurate formula can be used when the distance off is 5 miles or less: Distance off (in miles) equals the object's height (in feet) times .565 divided by the vertical angle (in minutes). Sextant errors must be corrected, and if observing a lighthouse, use the height of its light. The observer should be reasonably close to sea level and the height of tide must be considered.

—A *bow-beam bearing* can be used when passing an object to determine distance off without the need to plot on the chart. Take a bearing when the object you are passing is 45 degrees on the bow. Then hold the boat on a steady course until the object bears 90 degrees. At that point

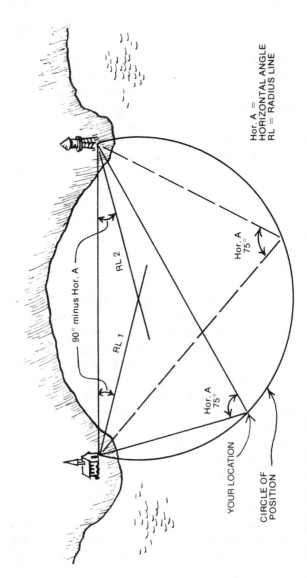

Hor. A =
HORIZONTAL ANGLE
RL = RADIUS LINE

90° minus Hor. A

RL 2

RL 1

Hor. A
75°

Hor. A
75°

YOUR LOCATION

CIRCLE OF
POSITION

Fig. 6-10. Circle of position

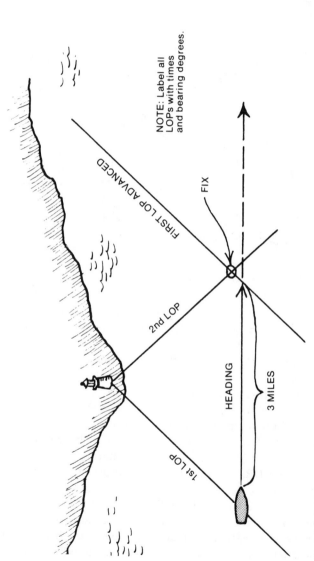

NOTE: Label all LOPs with times and bearing degrees.

FIRST LOP ADVANCED

2nd LOP

1st LOP

FIX

HEADING

3 MILES

Fig. 6-11. Running fix

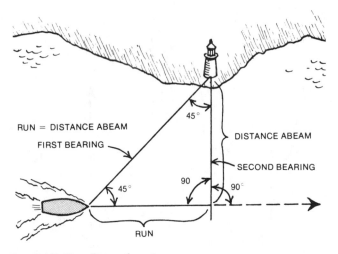

Fig. 6-12. Bow-beam bearing

your distance off will be equal to your run (the distance between bearings determined by dead reckoning). See illustration.

—*Doubling the angle on the bow* is also a geometrical method of figuring (without the need to plot) your distance away from an object you are passing. As shown in the sample illustration, a bearing is taken from a distance when approaching the object (25 degrees in the example) and then a steady course is held until the object's bearing has doubled (50 degrees). At this time the run, determined by DR, is equal to the distance away from the object.

—Special cases of doubling the angle are the ⁷/₈ *rule* and the ⁷/₁₀ *rule*. Using these rules, the distance from the object when it bears abeam (at 90 degrees to the heading) is a fraction of the run. When the bearings are 30 and then

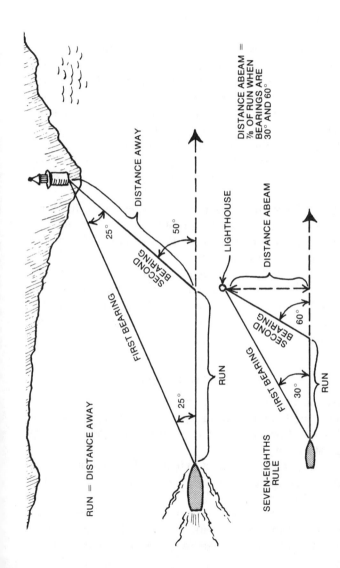

RUN = DISTANCE AWAY

DISTANCE AWAY

DISTANCE AWAY

25°

50°

25°

FIRST BEARING

SECOND BEARING

RUN

DISTANCE ABEAM = 7/8 OF RUN WHEN BEARINGS ARE 30° AND 60°

LIGHTHOUSE

DISTANCE ABEAM

60°

SECOND BEARING

FIRST BEARING

RUN

30°

SEVEN-EIGHTHS RULE

Fig. 6-13. Doubling the angle on the bow

60 degrees, distance to the object is seven-eighths of the
run; and when the bearings are 22½ and then 45 degrees, the distance is seven-tenths of the run.

— *Beam rounding* is a method of safely rounding a point
that has a prominant landmark at its end. Head for the
object until close to shoal water at the end of the point
(determined after a study of the chart). To make a semi-
circular rounding that keeps the course a safe distance
off, keep the object exactly abeam (bearing 90 degrees
from dead ahead). This will prevent you from inadvertently creeping close to the shoal projecting from the
point's end.

— Distance to the horizon can be determined by taking
the square root of your height of eye above the waterline
in feet and multiplying it by 1.17. This gives the distance
to the visible horizon in nautical miles.

— Distance to a lighthouse (or other tall object whose
height is on the chart), as seen when its top first appears
above the horizon, is obtained by adding your distance to
the horizon to 1.17 times the square root of the lighthouse's height.

DEAD RECKONING

Most navigation texts say that the word "dead" in dead
reckoning is derived from the abbreviation of "deduced"
(although Bowditch literally interpreted "dead" as meaning "stationary").

At any rate, DR is used to figure a boat's position with
the use of speed in knots (S) multiplied by time (T) to
obtain distance (D):

— $S \times T = D$. Divide $S \times T$ (in minutes) by 60 when minutes
are needed in timing a run. This formula is easy to use,
but some pilots prefer to use a speed-time-distance calcu-

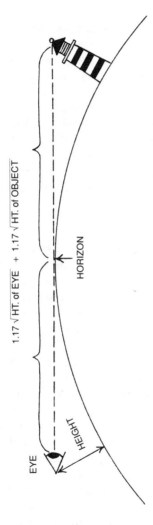

$1.17 \sqrt{\text{HT. of EYE}} + 1.17 \sqrt{\text{HT. of OBJECT}}$

HORIZON

EYE

HEIGHT

Fig. 6-14. Distance to a tall object first seen above the horizon

lator, a logarithmic speed scale, or tables (found in navigation books).

—Knotmeters and logs can be checked for accuracy by running a measured mile (between markers or ranges that are exactly one mile apart). When no measured mile is available, use markers or buoys whose distance apart is easy to work with: a distance that is to the exact tenth of a mile and no less than $\frac{4}{10}$ of a mile nor more than 1 mile. Run the course in both directions and average speeds to allow for current, wind, and waves. Sight each buoy or marker when it is exactly abeam, and time your run with a stopwatch. Use the S × T = D formula, but in the following form which is modified for timing in seconds:

$$S = \frac{D \times 3600}{T \text{ (in sec.)}}$$

—If you have no knotmeter or log, reasonably accurate speed can be estimated with a tachometer, which shows the engine's revolutions per minute (RPMs). You will have to make the measured mile runs, as described above, for a broad range of commonly used RPMs. From this information a speed curve can be drawn on graph paper to show speed at all RPMs.

—The *Dutchman's log* is another method of finding out your speed. An object, such as a scrap of wood or wad of paper, is thrown overboard at the bow, the stopwatch is started when the object hits the water, and the watch is stopped when the object is abeam at the stern. Sixty percent of the boat's length is divided by the number of seconds on the watch to give the speed in knots. If the timing were four seconds on a 37 footer, her speed would be 22.2 divided by 4 or 5.55 knots. The object should be thrown overboard at least 3 feet away from the boat so that it will not be affected by the water flow around the hull.

— Speed can be figured in a similar way when passing close to a buoy. The bow person shouts when the buoy is abeam, and the person aft immediately starts the watch, then stops it when the buoy comes abeam of his or her location. Again, 60 percent of the distance (between persons) is divided by the time in seconds to obtain the speed in knots.

— The 6-Minute Rule is a quick and handy means of estimating your DR position. The distance a boat travels in 6 minutes equals her speed divided by 10. For example, a speed of 4 knots in 6 minutes will produce a distance of .4 miles.

— DR does not take into account the effects of current and leeway, so these factors must be considered before you can obtain a more accurate "estimated position."

— Current information can be obtained from tidal current tables or current charts, but a wise practice is to observe constantly the flow of water around buoys or channel markers. In conditions of poor visibility and calm wind, you can anchor temporarily and use the above-described Dutchman's log technique to find the speed of the current.

— Leeway can be estimated in a rough way by sighting aft on your wake and noting how far it is from being dead astern.

— The *60 formula* is useful in figuring a heading when the current is on your beam. To correct for the sidewise push of the current, divide 60 by the course length (the length of your run) and multiply by the number of miles the current will set you off course. The result provides the number of degrees off course you must steer to compensate for the current. Let us suppose you are headed north on a 15-mile course and figure that during the time of your run the current will set you 3 miles to the west; divide 60 by

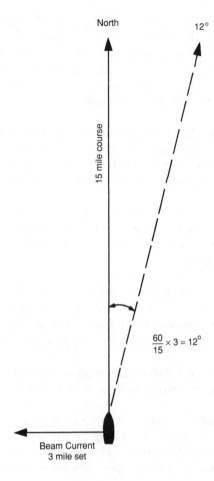

North

12°

15 mile course

$$\frac{60}{15} \times 3 = 12°$$

Beam Current
3 mile set

Fig. 6-15. The 60 formula

15 and multiply by 3 to obtain 12, the number of degrees east of north you must steer to compensate.

—When the current set is 45 degrees from the plotted course, multiply the 60 formula result by $\frac{2}{3}$. When the set is 30 degrees from the course, multiply the result by $\frac{1}{2}$.

ELECTRONIC PILOTING

Electronic navigational instruments can be extremely helpful in fog or other conditions of poor visibility, but the navigator should not totally depend on them, as most are subject to inaccuracies or occasional failures due to loss of electrical power, water saturation, corrosion, atmospheric conditions, interference, imperfect installation, damage to antennas or transducers, etc. Always check electronic findings against the more basic systems such as visual bearings, ranges, vertical angles, and DR. It has often been said that the prudent navigator never depends solely on one source of navigational information.

Depth-Sounders

Often called echo sounders or fathometers, depth sounders determine water depth by sending downward ultrasonic waves from a transducer near the boat's bottom to the seabed. These waves are reflected back to the transducer and their time of travel is converted to depth and shown on a display module which may be in the form of a digital, analog, or flashing light indicator, video display screen, or recording device. A few miscellaneous tips for selection, installation, and use are:

—Depth-sounders that may be used for fish finding are generally more difficult to read and interpret than single purpose sounders with digital or analog displays.

— Flashing-light sounders (with a rotating arm that emits flashes at zero and bottom depth on the indicator's circular scale) can provide information about the seabed (whether it is hard or soft, etc.). However, these sounders may need sun shades and frequent adjustment of the sensitivity control.

— When any kind of sounder shows two or more depths, it is the safest policy to assume that the shallowest reading is correct.

— Transducers that are mounted fairly close to amidships are usually most efficient, since they are well clear of aerated water from the vessel's bow wave and wake.

— Amidships external transducers usually require a fairing block that will level the transducer so that it can send its beam of sound waves directly downward. Sailboats with high angles of heel must have their transducers mounted well below the waterline, and they sometimes need one on each side.

— The transducer's beam width must be fairly wide on a sailboat so that the sound waves will be sent, as much as possible, directly downward when the boat heels.

— Be sure you know the depth of your transducer and the distance between it and the bottom of your keel. Remember that unless you have a sounder that can be set to correct for the difference between transducer and keel depth, the depth reading will be from the transducer to seabed. The depth you are concerned with is obviously the depth under the deepest part of your keel.

— Internal transducers (those mounted inside the bilge) are often used on racing sailboats primarily to reduce drag. These have proven satisfactory on many uncored fiberglass boats but at some cost in efficiency. Quite often, for improved performance, internal transducers are mounted in cofferdams (oil- or water-filled chambers in-

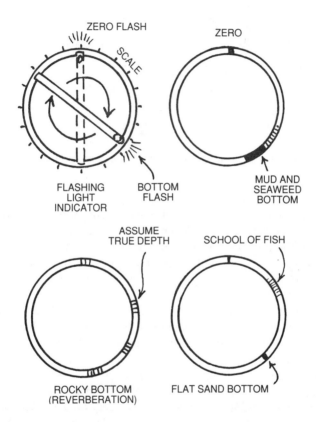

Fig. 6-16. Interpretation of a flashing light depth sounder

side the hull) so that the sound waves can begin their travel through liquid.
—A handy feature on most depth sounders is an alarm that may be set to sound off when the boat reaches shal-

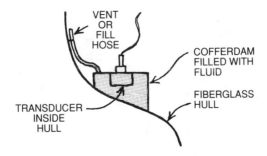

Fig. 6-17. A cofferdam for internal depth-sounder

low water. Set the alarm a few feet deeper than the draft
of the boat for ample warning to avoid a grounding.
—Running a fathom line is one technique of piloting in
reduced visibility with a depth-sounder. Steer a slightly
weaving course closely following a fathom line shown on
the chart that connects all points of equal depth. When
your depth changes on the indicator, turn the boat until
the reading again corresponds with the depth marked on
the fathom line. Repeat the process each time the depth
changes.
—A *chain of soundings* can also help establish your position in foggy weather. This involves a series of soundings
taken at regular intervals (perhaps every quarter mile) on
a straight course at a fixed rate of moderately slow speed.
Plot your course and soundings on a piece of tracing paper, lay the paper on the chart, orient it to the direction
you are steering, and move it around until your soundings correspond to those on the chart.
—Carry a lead-line or the equivalent (a marked line with
weight) as a backup for the depth-sounder.

Radio Direction Finder

Despite more accurate, modern electronic systems of navigation, which are more constantly usable and often easier to use, radio direction finding is still popular mainly because of its low cost and low electrical drain. There should be a number of marine radio beacons in your area for the most effective RDF navigation, but even one beacon can be helpful to home on (head directly for) or obtain an LOP, bow beam bearing, or running fix. The typical, portable RDF receiver carried on a small boat is battery-powered with a rotatable ferrite bar antenna that reads against a 360 degree azimuth scale. When the antenna is rotated, there is a change in strength of the signal coming from the radio beacon.

—To obtain a bearing from a radio beacon, turn the antenna until you reach a null, where the signal is weakest. The antenna (or pointer) will then be pointing directly (or nearly so) toward or away from the beacon.

—There are actually two nulls about 180 degrees apart. In the unlikely event that you are confused about which null you want, turn the boat about beam to the signal and proceed until the bearing changes, and then it should be apparent in which direction the beacon lies. Some receivers have a sense antenna to help with this problem.

—The RDF receiver should be equipped with a nullmeter so that the nulls can be determined not only audibly but also visibly (with the meter's needle pointing at the low end of the scale).

—Before locating the null, turn the antenna until the nullmeter's needle points to the high end of the scale in order to obtain maximum volume for ease in identifying the signal.

— Radio beacons send out their signals in Morse code, which is shown on standard charts, in the government publication *Light Lists*, or in publication 117 *Radio Navigational Aids* (published by the Defense Mapping Agency Hydrographic/Topographic Center) for foreign waters.

— Marine radio beacons usually send their signals continuously but some are sequential with several taking turns operating on the same frequency. The latter type are marked on the charts with Roman numerals indicating the sequence of transmission. Details can be found in the *Light Lists*.

— Beacon signals are marked on charts with dots and dashes; therefore it is not essential to know the Morse code. However, knowing the code can be helpful, because the letters of the alphabet formed by the dots and dashes often relate to the location they identify. When the author made a landfall at Faial in the Azores, for example, he picked up a strong signal FIL (for Faial), which was not listed in the current edition of publication 117.

— RDF is subject to deviation like the magnetic compass, therefore the error should be checked by comparing the radio bearing with the visual bearing of a beacon when there is good visibility. A deviation card similar to that for the compass can be made for the RDF. Always operate the

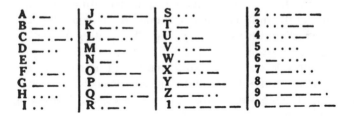

Fig. 6-18. Morse code

Fig. 6-19. Portable RDF with ferrite antenna

RDF receiver from the same location it was in when the deviation card was made.

— To minimize deviation, keep the radio as far as possible from ferrous objects and electric wires. Continuous metal lifelines can cause errors that might be alleviated by fastening the lifelines to the bow and stern pulpits with rope lashings.

—RDF navigation is less accurate at night and least accurate at dawn and dusk. Accuracy is also decreased when the radio waves cross a shoreline at oblique angles.

— Some high-powered radio beacons can be received from distances of up to 200 miles, but the closer you are to a beacon the better your chance of an accurate bearing.

—A few marine beacons send synchronized sound and radio signals. With this type, the navigator can time the difference between the two signals and calculate how far he or she is from the beacon. The distance in nautical miles can be figured by dividing the time difference by 5.5.

—To obtain a magnetic bearing, align the RDF receiver's azimuth scale with the boat's centerline (zero degree pointed at the bow), and the boat's compass heading is obtained from the helmsman when the bearing is taken. Then add the heading to the relative bearing (measured clockwise from the bow). If the addition exceeds 360 degrees, 360 is subtracted to obtain the bearing from magnetic north. Handheld RDFs carry their own compasses, which are usually less accurate than the vessel's steering compass.

—Most commercial AM radio stations and aeronautical beacons can be used for direction finding, but you must know the location of their transmitting antennas, and they should be near the coast for greatest accuracy.

Radar

Despite certain disadvantages, radar (the acronym for radio detecting and ranging) is an extremely valuable tool in foggy regions. The disadvantages include cost; the need to interpret and frequently tune; the necessity of a fairly large heavy, rotating, transceiving antenna; inaccuracy due to heeling and rolling; and high electrical demands. As with other electronic gear, however, improvements are constantly being made to increase suitability for small craft.

Two major advantages of radar over other forms of radio navigation is that the navigator is provided with a special kind of bird's eye picture of the surroundings on a screen or scope called a plan position indicator (PPI). Although this is not the same picture shown on a chart, it clearly shows bold shores, buoys, and other vessels in the immediate vicinity. The other advantage is that radar emits its own radio pulses (at ultra-high frequencies) and therefore will never be affected by lack of coverage as are many other systems which depend on remote radio transmissions.

The maximum range of radar depends on the power of its transmitter and height of its antenna, as well as the height of the target. A satisfactory range for all practical purposes, considering suitability for piloting and collision avoidance, is about 12 miles, but many small boats have to settle for less.

The following suggestions may be helpful to those getting started with radar:

— Although height of the antenna is important for maximum range, don't install it too high, as the altitude will adversely affect minimum range (imparing its ability to detect nearby objects) and heeling/rolling errors will be magnified.

— Mount the scanner (antenna) well above the head level of standing crew, as radar transmitters emit radiation similar to microwaves (sea gulls have been "cooked" by radar transmissions). Avoid direct exposure by at least 4 feet.

— The circular, enclosed scanner known as a radome is generally satisfactory for mast mounting on a sailboat, as the radome is relatively light and its size and rounded shape minimize fouling lines or sails. A good mounting spot is the mizzen of a yawl or ketch, but the mast may need to be stronger than normal.

— Special masts or arches are often used aft to mount the scanner, and some mounts are self-leveling or may be adjusted manually to allow for heel. The antenna starts to become ineffective when the heeling angle exceeds 12 degrees.

— Despite producing a somewhat jagged picture, raster scan radar provides a continual picture that does not fade out during the antenna's sweep. Beginners usually find it easier to work with a steady picture.

— In tuning the radar, adjust the gain control to amplify returns for distant targets, but use less amplification for targets that are close by. Use the large range scale for distant objects but small scale for a clearer picture of close objects.

— The sea clutter (caused by returns from steep seas) can obscure targets, but can be minimized by adjustment of the STC (sensitivity time control). Too low a setting may obscure close objects.

— The rain clutter control, FTC (fast time constant), can be adjusted to help prevent precipitation from obscuring targets. However, it is often helpful to keep the FTC turned low during the night at sea when you are watching for approaching squalls.

Fig. 6-20. Self-leveling radar antenna (note method of towing dinghy to inhibit yawing)

—When interpreting the picture on the screen, bear in mind the following: Strong returns (readily appearing on the screen) are produced by targets that are close, large, high, and those composed of metal or flat rock and that are perpendicular to the radar beam. Bold coasts, high mountains, metal ships, and navigation aids or vessels with radar reflectors generally make good targets; whereas low shores, sloping beaches, marshes, and rounded objects make relatively poor targets.

—Whenever possible, when navigating with radar, plot your position. On large vessels the plots may be done on special plotting sheets or a maneuvering board, but on a small boat it is usually best to plot directly on your chart. Compare the picture on the radar screen with your area on the chart.

— Keep in mind that your position on the radar screen is at its center and your heading is at the top of the screen, zero degrees on the azimuth circle enclosing the radar returns.

— Bearings are read by moving a cursor called the EBL (electronic bearing line) which can be swung around the screen to the object on which you are taking the bearing. Distance to the object is read by moving the VRM (variable range marker), an electronic circle that expands from the screen's center, to the object. A fix is obtained when the EBL and VRM cross the object.

— In areas where there are many buoys there may be a racon (radar beacon), which is easily identifiable since it sends a return that shows up on your radar screen either as a radial line extending toward the edge of the screen or as a letter in Morse code. The letter would show as a line of dots and dashes on the far side of the target.

— A valuable tool to the shorthanded sailor is a radar detector, an instrument of low power drainage which sounds an alarm when an approaching vessel is using radar. These devices are often mounted on the stern pulpit, and some types will show the relative bearing of the approaching vessel.

— Be sure to read your radar instruction manual carefully, and practice using your set in clear weather so that you can compare the screen picture with the actual view.

— As mentioned earlier, every small vessel in foggy weather should carry a radar reflector. For best reflection the open type should be displayed in the "rain catch" position (with one of the cavities facing upward, appearing to have the capability of holding water). Bear in mind,

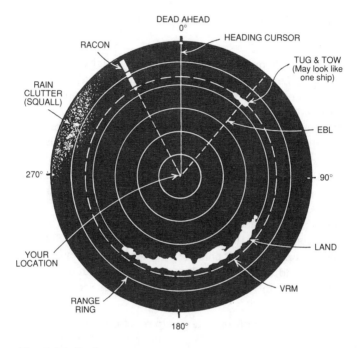

Fig. 6-21. Radar screen

DEAD AHEAD 0°
HEADING CURSOR
RACON
TUG & TOW (May look like one ship)
RAIN CLUTTER (SQUALL)
EBL
270°
90°
YOUR LOCATION
LAND
RANGE RING
VRM
180°

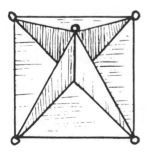

Fig. 6-22. Radar reflector in rain catch position

however, that even if a vessel has its radar operating, there might not be a continuous radar watch.

Loran-C

Second in popularity to RDF and only slightly more expensive, Loran-C (acronym for long range navigation) is an automatic, low frequency (100 KHz) pulsed radio navigational system that provides hyperbolic (curved) LOPs. Chains of widely-spaced, land-based transmitters send synchronized pulses at precise time intervals, and the onboard receiver measures time differences (TDs) in microseconds (ms, millionths of a second) between the arrival time of the transmissions. Each chain has a master station and several secondaries (formerly called slaves). A TD between the master and a secondary is displayed on the Loran screen in the form of a five-digit number. This is plotted on a Loran-C chart (a standard chart over-printed with a grid of hyperbolic lines) as an LOP. Another LOP, obtained from TDs of another secondary, is required for a fix.

—Tune to the appropriate group repetition interval (GRI) which is the total elapsed time between a chain's master signals (shown as a four-digit number identifying the chain), and then obtain TDs from the best secondaries. The Loran normally does this automatically.

—If the secondaries are selected manually rather than automatically, select a strong station and one with a wide crossing angle (as close as possible to 90 degrees) to minimize plotting errors.

—The secondary grids shown on a Loran-C chart are hyperbolic LOPs marked with TDs and labeled W (with lines colored blue), X (magenta), Y (black), and Z (green). LOPs printed on the chart show where the TDs are constant.

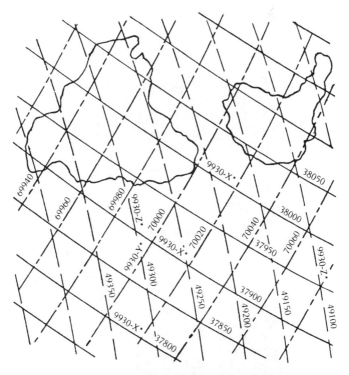

Fig. 6-23. TD grid on a Loran-C chart (Based on a sample in Loran-C User Handbook, *published by the U.S. Coast Guard.)*

—Your position will usually fall somewhere between the printed LOPs, since the five-digit microsecond number shown on the Loran screen will seldom coincide exactly with the microsecond numbers printed on the chart. Therefore, interpolation will probably be necessary. This can be done with dividers and the linear plotter printed on

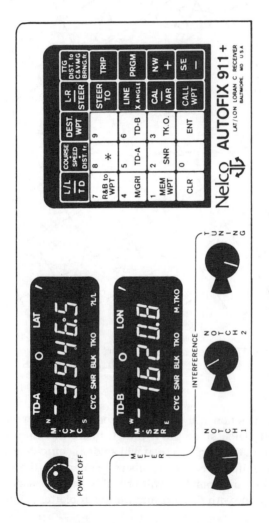

Fig. 6-24. Nelco Autoflex 911 Loran receiver (Courtesy Nelco)

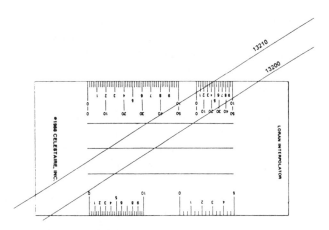

Fig. 6-25. Loran plotter (Courtesy Celestaire Navigation Instruments)

the Loran-C chart or with a Loran-C plotter (see illustration).

—The need to plot your position can be avoided at some small cost in accuracy by converting TDs to a latitude/longitude readout. Your position can then be found on a standard chart, but Loran charts should be carried in case you need greater accuracy or to confirm your position with TDs.

—Loran is subject to several errors, including those caused by thunderstorms, interference from powerful radio stations (near 100 KHz), and land effects (when the signals pass over land) known as ASFs (additional secondary phase factors). Furthermore, Loran is subject to interference from other radio signals, motors, and fluorescent lights (they should be turned off when Loran is operating). Notch filters in the receiver will help with signal interference.

— Most modern Lorans can automatically correct for ASF, but because of this error, TD lines are not printed on harbor charts, and Loran should not be considered dependable on inshore waters. Never extend the printed TDs into inland waters.

— For most effective use a Loran needs a proper antenna (one recommended by the manufacturer) mounted away from metal rigging and other antennas, and the receiver should be grounded. Handheld Lorans have some advantages, but suffer from a small antenna and lack of grounding.

— When signal strengths are weak the Loran receiver will blink or flash the display. This warns the navigator that he or she should shift to another station with a stronger signal (provided its LOP has a satisfactory crossing angle).

— The most reliable range for Loran results from ground-wave (close to the ground) reception and covers from 1000 to 1200 nautical miles. Reception from fringe areas (at the end of this range) and from sky-waves (radiation reflected off the ionosphere) at a far greater range may be in error by a couple of miles or more.

— Loran "crash" (loss of memory, inaccuracy, etc.) can occur when the Loran is operating during a momentary power interruption. Do not operate during a thunderstorm or when starting the engine, or else buy a surge protector such as the Newmar Nav-Pac.

— Loran is not a worldwide system, but coverage is very good on both coasts of the United States and the Great Lakes.

— Loran accuracy can be checked by positioning the boat at a fixed marker (an offshore lighthouse, for example) whose latitude and longitude are known and then comparing the Loran's reading. Be aware that buoys can be slightly off station.

Global Positioning System (GPS)

The Global Positioning System (GPS), based on very high frequency signals sent from groups of satellites, is the most accurate and easy to use radio navigation system. It has all but replaced the older satellite system known as satnav, which had at least one serious drawback in that there were only a few transmitting satellites, and the navigator was forced to wait (as long as several hours in some cases) between satellite passes. GPS, however, uses multiple high-altitude satellites (presently nineteen) and therefore provides a continuous worldwide system. Largely unaffected by land effects and range limitations, GPS achieves extremely accurate and reliable positions through ranging and triangulation with time differences (like Loran).

—A GPS receiver is relatively unaffected by electrical interference, and it only requires a small antenna, but one that should have open sky above and around it.

—Unlike Loran, there is no need to plot on a special chart and interpolate for greatest accuracy. Very accurate latitude and longitude, obtained from the GPS display screen, is simply plotted on a standard chart.

—About the only disadvantages of GPS, compared with Loran, are cost (although costs are rapidly decreasing); lack of ability to check signal strength (failure to blink); and deliberate signal degradation, (called SA for selective availability), by the Department of Defense for national security reasons.

—GPS for civilian use has been degraded by the Department of Defense to about 100 meters (328.1 ft.) of positional accuracy. However, differential GPS, which makes

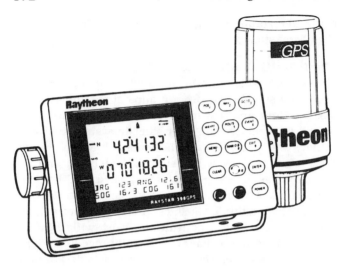

Fig. 6-26. Raystar 390 GPS (Courtesy of Raytheon and Coast Navigation)

use of shore signals in addition to those from satellites, has improved accuracy to within 10 meters (32.8 ft.).

—Although every electronic navigator should have non-electrical backup systems in case there is a loss of power, there are highly accurate portable GPS receivers that operate on small alkaline (AA) batteries and spares can be carried. You'd better carry plenty of spares, though, because the small batteries only last for about 6 to 10 hours. Some single channel portables may have a "sleep mode" (operating only when absolutely necessary) to conserve power.

—Handheld GPS receivers need to be reasonably water-proof because they will often be operated from the cockpit where integral antennas should have clear sky. If operated from belowdecks, a handheld should be plugged into a fixed external antenna.

AIDS TO NAVIGATION

Most waters used by boats are marked with aids to navigation in the form of anchored buoys, fixed channel markers, ranges (short and tall markers some distance apart that can be aligned), beacons, and lighthouses. Many of these aids are numbered, some are lighted, and some are equipped with sound or radio signals. On U.S. federally controlled waters, aids are placed according to the IALA-B lateral system (IALA stands for International Association of Lighthouse Authorities). Under this system the port side of a channel, as seen when entering from seaward, is marked with green aids having odd numbers, and the starboard side is marked with even-numbered red aids. The well known mnemoic for remembering this system is "Red, Right, Returning." In some foreign waters (in northern Europe, for example) the opposite, IALA-A system is used, whereby red is kept to port and green to starboard when returning.

—The basic types of unlighted buoys for U.S. waters are shown in the accompanying illustration. Notice that they have different shapes to help with identification. Cylindrical shaped buoys called cans are green and they mark the port side of the channel (when entering), while conic buoys (those with a tapered or pointed top) called nuns are red and they mark the channel's starboard side.

—Daymarks (fixed aids normally consisting of geometric dayboards on pilings) use square green boards for the port side of a channel and red triangular boards for the starboard side (when returning).

unlighted buoys without sound

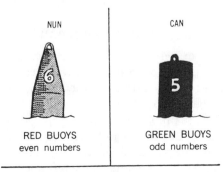

NUN

CAN

RED BUOYS
even numbers

GREEN BUOYS
odd numbers

MID-CHANNEL BUOYS
red and white vertical stripes

preferred channel
lies to port (returning)

preferred channel
to starboard (returning)

NUN

CAN

JUNCTION OR OBSTRUCTION BUOYS
red and green horizontal bands

Fig. 6-27. U.S. Buoy system (IALA-B Lateral)

— Midchannel buoys, which indicate that you should pass fairly close on either side, are either rounded in shape or else they have round top marks. They are marked with red and white vertical bands. Daymarks have octagonal red and white boards.

— Buoys that have horizontal bands of red and green are junction or obstruction markers (sometimes called middle ground buoys). They can be passed on either side, but the shape (can or nun) and color of the topmost band indicates the side on which the preferred channel lies. Daymarks use square and triangular boards.

— Buoys are marked on a chart with elongated diamond shapes above a dot which pinpoints the buoy's location. It should be kept in mind, however, that an anchored buoy's position is almost never exact, and it may be moved a moderate distance by severe storms or ice.

— Nighttime identification of lighted navigational aids is made possible by individual light characteristics. For example, some aids have flashing (quick, slow, group) or occulting lights, and these might be colored red, green, white, or yellow. The accompanying figure shows the various light rhythms with their symbols (shown on the chart) and meanings.

— Other U.S. navigational aids include Intracoastal Waterway (ICW) markers and the Uniform State Waterway Marking System (USWMS). Both of these systems are quite similar to the federal system.

— The main differences between IALA-B and USWMS are that black takes the place of green, and occasionally a cardinal plan is used as follows: A white buoy with red top means a boat should pass to the south or west of it, while a buoy with a black top means the boat should pass to the north or east of it. A buoy with red and white vertical stripes warns that an obstruction exists, and the boat

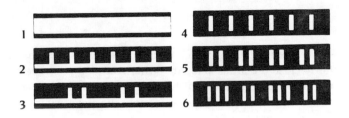

	SYMBOLS AND MEANINGS		
	Lights which do not change color	**Lights which show color variations**	**PHASE DESCRIPTION**
1	F.=Fixed -------------	Alt.=Alternating.	A continuous steady light.
2	F.Fl.=Fixed and flashing.	Alt.F.Fl.=Alternating fixed and flashing.	A fixed light varied at regular intervals by a single flash of greater brilliance.
3	F.Gp.Fl.=Fixed and group flashing.	Alt.F.Gp.Fl.=Alternating fixed and group flashing.	A fixed light varied at regular intervals by groups of 2 or more flashes of greater brilliance. The group may, or may not, be preceded and followed by an eclipse.
4	Fl.=Flashing---------	Alt.Fl.=Alternating flashing.	Showing a single flash at regular intervals, the duration of light always being less than the duration of darkness.
5	Gp.Fl.=Group flashing.	Alt.Gp.Fl.=Alternating group flashing.	Showing at regular intervals groups of 2 or more flashes.
6	Gp.Fl.(3+2)=Composite group flashing.	--------------------------	Group flashing in which the flashes are combined in alternate groups of different numbers.

Fig. 6-28. Light rhythms of navigation aids (From the Coast Guard Light Lists)

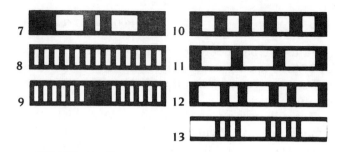

	SYMBOLS AND MEANINGS		
	Lights which do not change color	**Lights which show color variations**	**PHASE DESCRIPTION**
7	**Mo.(K)**=Morse Code.	--------------------	Light in which flashes of different durations are grouped to produce a Morse *character* or *characters*.
8	**Qk.Fl.**=Quick flashing.	--------------------	Shows not less than 60 flashes per minute.
9	**Int.(I)Qk.Fl.**= Interrupted quick flashing.	--------------------	Shows quick flashes for about 4 seconds, followed by a dark period of about 4 seconds.
10	**Iso.(E.Int.)**=Equal intervals.	--------------------	Duration of light equal to that of darkness.
11	**Occ.**=Occulting.	**Alt.Occ.**=Alternating occulting.	A light totally eclipsed at regular intervals, the duration of light always greater than the duration of darkness.
12	**Gp.Occ.**=Group occulting.	**Alt.Gp.Occ.**=Alternating group occulting.	A light with a group of 2 or more eclipses at regular intervals.
13	**Gp.Occ.(3+4)**= Composite group occulting.	--------------------	Group occulting in which the occultations are combined in alternate groups of different numbers.

Fig. 6-28. (Continued)

should not pass between it and the nearest shore. USWMS is usually found in state waters not open to the sea and not connected to the sea by navigable rivers or channels.

The ICW uses a plan similar to the IALA-B lateral system, but "entering from seaward" is considered the same as proceeding to the south and west. A mnemonic is "sea green and red clay" meaning that red is on the shore side and green on the sea's side. Confusion can occur, however, because some aids along the ICW are dual purpose where, for example, a river might cross the ICW. Aids that mark the ICW have small yellow squares or triangles, and these should govern in cases of ambiguity. A yellow triangle indicates that the aid should be left to starboard when proceeding to the south or west, while a yellow square is left to port.

—Additional markers found on U.S. waters are informational or regulatory markers. These are white with orange markings. Messages are conveyed either with writing, such as "clam line," or a symbol. Important symbols are: a diamond, meaning danger; a cross inside a diamond, meaning a prohibited area; and a circle, meaning restricted operations. Special-purpose aids, to mark fishnet or dredging areas, etc., are yellow. A mooring buoy is white with a horizontal blue band.

—Whenever there is doubt about the meaning of a navigational aid consult your chart or light list.

7. Emergencies

*Any small boat sailor standing out past the sea
buoy should be a little frightened. Those who seldom experience fear may substitute the term height-
ened awareness. This is part of the thrill of boating.
At sea there is a sensible channel between excess
complacency and undue anxiety.*
          — *Captain John M. Waters, Jr., USCG (Ret.)*

It might be argued that the expert seaman should rarely if
ever be faced with an emergency, but this argument is not
valid for at least two reasons: First, there is no such thing
as a perfect seaman—no one is above making an occasional mistake. Let experienced sailors brag about being
infallible, and the chances are they will find themselves
in trouble the very next day. Second, no one can predict
with certainty when an accident will occur; a metal fitting
might have an internal flaw, other gear or rigging that
looks sound could break, or the weather might turn foul
despite favorable predictions. Obviously, every boater
should do his best to avoid an emergency, but should
always be prepared. Preparation includes anticipation
(imagining everything that could possibly go wrong), forethought about coping with any kind of adversity, and attention to equipping the boat with safety gear that will
help prevent or deal with an emergency. General safety
equipment has already been covered in Chapter 1, but
this chapter will include a few more specialized items

and further details on gear already mentioned. Forethought helps avoid panic, which is the greatest liability in dealing with any kind of crisis.

The most frequent kinds of emergencies with which the average boater may be faced are: swamping or capsizing, running aground, engine failure, fouling the propeller or underwater appendages, rigging failure, person overboard, personal injury, serious leaks, steering failure, collisions, and fire.

SWAMPING OR CAPSIZING

— Swamping is most likely in a small, open boat. To avoid swamping don't overload. Keep ample freeboard, especially when the waters are choppy. See that your boat has ample flotation.

— Beware of swamping when the boat is trimmed down by the stern and there is a cutaway transom to accomodate a short shaft outboard motor. As noted in Chapter 4, this arrangement needs a watertight, self-draining well just forward of the motor.

— If shipping water over the bow when underway, slow down and slightly elevate the bow with crew weight, trim tabs, or motor tilt.

— Keep crew weight close to amidships and as low as possible in a small open boat (don't stand up or suddenly move to one side).

— Think twice about anchoring by the stern, especially when freeboard aft is low and there is no afterdeck. This is particularly risky on a boat with a flat vertical transom, which encourages waves to splash over the stern.

— Don't allow water to accumulate in the bilge. Be sure there is a large, sturdy bucket and adequate pumps on large boats (see Chapter 1).

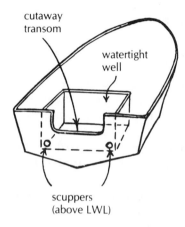

cutaway transom

watertight well

scuppers (above LWL)

Fig. 7-1. Outboard motor well

— To avoid swamping, a dinghy being towed should always be brought aboard the mother vessel well before the beginning of bad weather. When shorthanded and lacking davits (lifting devices), a dinghy often can be hoisted aboard with a winch servicing a halyard that is secured to the middle of a bridle attached to the dinghy's bow and stern.

— Before beginning to bail a swamped boat, try to remove some water by sloshing it out. If you can, give repeated quick pulls on the painter or bowline, which will cause the water to flow aft over the stern.

— When sailing a small centerboard boat in a breeze, never sit in an awkward position that could prevent your moving quickly. Always be ready to shift your weight instantly to the high side.

—When struck by a puff, be ready to slack sheets and/or to luff up if sailing close to the wind or to bear off if sailing on a broad reach.

—Keep good steerageway and be sure your sheets are free to run.

—In a strong wind, consider tacking rather than jibing to change tacks.

—Don't hesitate to reduce sail. Top up the end of the main boom to keep it from tripping (submerging its end), and reef the sail's leech to remove slack. (Reefing is discussed in Chapter 8.)

—If capsized, quickly stand on the centerboard protruding from the bottom to prevent turtling (turning upside down).

—If you can't right the boat immediately, don a life jacket (provided you are not already wearing one).

—When there is difficulty righting a capsized boat, try to turn her bow to the wind. It will be helpful if you can anchor and lower sail.

—Never tow a capsized boat until she has been righted.

—Perhaps the most important rule for the victim of a capsizing is to stay with the boat. Don't try to swim for that "nearby" shore if the boat remains afloat.

RUNNING AGROUND

Grounding is a common mishap for a deep draft sailboat in shoal waters. The best way to avoid a grounding is obviously to observe navigational aids and the state of the tide carefully, study your chart, keep track of your position, and use the depth-sounder (or lead-line). The following is some advice on getting unstuck after grounding:

—Turn towards deep water immediately after the keel touches bottom. A backed jib may help you turn.

—If you have grounded on a lee shore in a sailboat, lower sails at once to prevent being driven further aground.

—If grounded on a windward shore you can often use your sails to heel the boat, but be sure you are headed toward deep water.

—When the boat cannot be turned immediately after grounding she might be backed off under power. In most cases, put crew weight forward to lift the deepest part of the keel, which is usually aft. (Know the boat's under-water configuration).

—Backing should be done cautiously to assure that the engine is not overheating, the water intake is not clogged with sediment, and the rudder heel is not buried. Be sure the water intake is submerged.

—When backing fails, the boat might be turned by putting out an anchor off the bow with its line leading nearly perpendicular to the boat's fore and aft centerline. Do this with caution if the boat has a long keel with little drag (depth aft). Fin keel boats will pivot much more easily.

—After the boat has been turned toward deep water, she might be kedged off (pulled off with an anchor). Anchors are discussed in Chapter 9.

—After grounding in soft mud, the boat might be sallied (rolled from side to side) to break suction. This might be accomplished by quickly moving crew weight from side to side, perhaps while utilizing waves from passing or circling motorboats.

—Heeling is an effective way to free a grounded boat, because draft is reduced not only as a result of the keel not being vertical, but also because the heeled hull rolls out (rises) as a result of the physical need for additional immersed volume (caused by heeling) to equal emersed volume. The accompanying illustration shows the sections of immersed and emersed volumes as "in" and "out"

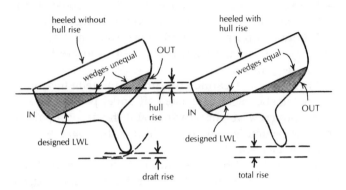

Fig. 7-2. Reduction of draft from rollout

wedges. Notice that the hull must rise to equalize the wedges.

—When sail cannot be used to induce heel, crew weight on one side can be used or a swamped dinghy can be lifted from the end of a broad-off boom.

—In stubborn cases, the boat can be heeled with a halyard run out to an anchor or another boat. Be aware, however, that the halyard block should be able to twist or swivel so that it can take a heavy load from the side.

—In the event of a centerboard boat running aground, of course her centerboard can be raised, but this should only be done when the wind and seas are driving the boat away from the shoal. Surprisingly, people don't always realize that when a shallow draft boat runs aground you can often step over the side and simply push the boat off the shoal.

—If grounded on rocks, inspect the hull carefully to see that it has not been holed. Otherwise, the boat could sink after being freed.

— If being pulled off by a powerboat, be sure the skipper of the towing boat knows where the deep water is. The towline should be fastened to a sturdy, through-bolted fitting or else fastened around the mast or even the entire hull. Never stand directly behind a towline in case it should part and whiplash. The towing boat should accelerate slowly to avoid shock loading.

— The degree and state of the tide is, of course, a major factor in a grounding emergency. When grounded on a high tide every effort should be made to extricate the boat immediately, but you may want to wait for the water to rise if you have run aground when the tide is low.

— In most U.S. waters there are semidiurnal tides (high and low waters occuring twice a lunar day [24 hours and 50 minutes]) with the tide changing every 6 hours and 12 minutes. Times and heights of high and low waters (at important reference stations) can be obtained from tide tables, and the state of the tide can often be judged by looking at watermarks along the shore or on pilings, etc.

— The *twelfths rule*, as shown in the accompanying diagram, is a rough means of determining when there will be the greatest tidal activity to assist or work against you when trying to free a grounded boat.

ENGINE FAILURE

As previously suggested, most powerboats that travel any distance should have a secondary means of propulsion (perhaps sails, oars, another engine, or an auxiliary outboard) in the event of primary engine failure. Lacking secondary power, there should be a means of calling for help (soon to be discussed). Immediately after a breakdown, of course, you should attempt repairs. By no means does the author claim to be a mechanic, but a great many

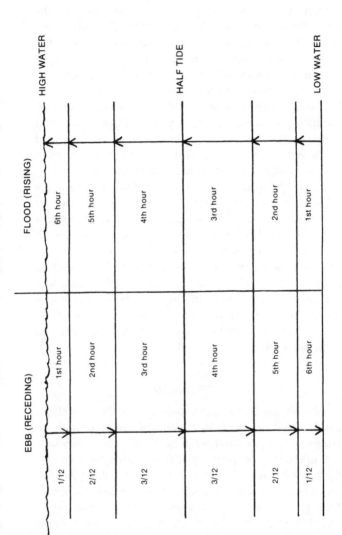

Fig. 7-3. *Twelfths rule for tide*

problems with engines (unless occurring suddenly and with much noise) are often easily overcome with simple remedies.

— To avoid engine problems be meticulous about maintenance (have a qualified mechanic do the servicing if you are not mechanically inclined) and be sure your fuel is clean.

— It is especially important that diesel fuel is free of dirt and water, as diesel engine injectors are particularly unforgiving. Filter the fuel as suggested in Chapter 4 and use a well respected marina or service station that pumps plenty of fuel. If in doubt about the quality of fuel, pour it into your tank through a screen from a semitransparent plastic bucket to allow prior examination for water and dirt. See that the tank's fill cap is screwed on tightly after fueling, and occasionally apply grease to the threads for waterproofing.

— Have ample filters on your fuel line and change them regularly. On a diesel fuel line there should be at least a primary filter, normally with a see-through bowl to trap water and large dirt particles, and a secondary filter to catch smaller material. Bear in mind that when filters are changed the fuel system has to be purged of air (bleeding instructions should be in your engine manual).

— The bottoms of fuel tanks should be pumped or drained periodically to remove water or sediment. Engine failure on a rough day may result from bottom sediment being stirred up and sucked into the fuel line. If you have a sailboat, sail into calm waters, and wait for the sediment and water to settle on the tank's bottom.

— Occasionally use a fuel soluble microbiocide such as Racor to prevent the growth of bacteria in a diesel oil tank. Be sure the fluid does not contain alcohol.

—When there are twin engines, see that they have separate tanks and fuel systems to help assure that there will be at least one engine in operation.

—An occasional problem with gasoline as well as diesel engines after experiencing heavy weather is water in the cylinders which enters via the exhaust outlet. There should be a high loop in the after end of the exhaust line, a high loop with anti-siphon vent in the cooling water line, and preferably an exhaust shutoff valve near the exhaust outlet that can be closed when the engine is not running before the advent of heavy weather. To remove water from the cylinders of a diesel engine, turn it over slowly with a crank after decompression levers have been lifted or perhaps by using a wrench on the crankshaft or prop shaft.

—When a diesel engine with decompression levers is hard to start due to a weak battery, lift the levers and get the engine turning over fast (with starting motor or crank), then, with the throttle open, push down the levers.

—One trick for helping start the engine on a fast moving sailboat is to freewheel the propeller with the gear in neutral, and, while turning the engine over, shift the gear into forward to help "bump start" the engine.

—Diesel engines are often difficult to start in cold weather. Be sure to use your cold start device such as glowplug (as described in your engine manual). Anything you can do to heat the engine compartment, even using a light bulb or kerosene lantern, will be helpful.

—Booster fluid (containing ether) can effectively overcome difficult starting, but many authorities warn against its use because of possible harm to the engine. If booster fluid must be used, spray only a very modest amount into the diesel engine's air intake or spray it on a rag which is then held at the intake.

—Starting difficulties resulting from poor compression (developing gradually over a period of time) might be cured temporarily with a couple of squirts of oil into the cylinders via the air intakes (after the air filters have been removed). This will help seal the piston rings and restore compression.

—A less common cause of diesel engine starting difficulties is clogged air intakes. Remove the intake horns and check the filters. Be sure there is ample ventilation into the engine compartment.

—A rare but potentially dangerous diesel problem is a runaway engine, when RPMs cannot be slowed with the throttle. The engine might be stopped with the fuel stop switch, by shutting the fuel valve, or by lifting the compression levers. An extreme alternative is to stuff rags against the air intake. Before drastic action is taken, however, check the throttle linkage to see that it is still connected.

—Common causes of overheating are a clogged seawater intake strainer, broken impeller on the water pump, and a faulty thermostat. In the latter case, the thermostat might be removed. Impellers often can be replaced without great difficulty, so it is well worth carrying a spare. Water intakes occasionally become clogged with submerged plastic or other flotsam. In this case, try shutting down the engine and perhaps the flotsam will wash off. Be sure the water intake seacock is fully open.

—Other causes of overheating are from a deficient level of lube oil, engine overload, and the formation of carbon in the cylinders and exhaust pipe. To avoid the latter, frequently run the engine at reasonably high RPMs and under moderate load (in gear). Overload may be caused by towing large boats or having a rag, plastic, or a line wrapped around the propeller.

— A propeller wrap is often caused by running into lobster or crab trap buoys or the painters of towed dinghies. These problems can be avoided with a careful lookout and by shortening scope on the dinghy painter when backing down. In buoy-infested waters it may pay to add a spur to the propeller to cut buoy lines. A badly wrapped line will have to be cut with a serrated knife or hacksaw, but sometimes a line can be cleared by momentarily (just for an instant) reversing the engine or reversing the shaft by hand (with engine off).

— Although gasoline engines are more tolerant of dirty fuel, in contrast with diesel engines, they are dependent on electrical ignition systems which are particularly vulnerable to moisture. Do your best to keep the ignition system dry and all electrical connections clean and tight.

Fig. 7-4. A cutting spur for inhibiting propeller wraps on a barnacle-covered prop

—Beginning with the battery, keep its top clean, especially the terminals. Check the fluid level to assure that it is a quarter to a half inch above the plates. Check the battery state with a battery condition meter or hydrometer. Use a "make before break" battery selector switch and don't switch to off with the engine running unless the switch is an alternator field disconnect model.

—As a very general rule, the gradual failure of a running gasoline engine which sputters and hesitates is a fuel problem, but a sudden stopping (without clanking or grinding noises) indicates an electrical failure.

—When the engine cannot be started despite a healthy battery with tight cables and clean terminals, check the starter switch. See that connections to the solenoid are tight, and if they are, connect the solenoid's small terminal (for the ignition switch wire) with the large terminal (for the battery cable) using a jumper cable or screwdriver having an insulated handle. This will turn over the starting motor and perhaps start the engine when the switch is defective. (Note: a solenoid is a heavy duty electromechanial switch. It is mounted on top of a pre-engaged starting motor).

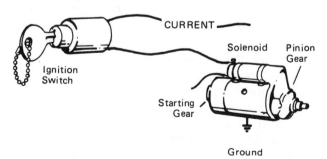

Fig. 7-5. Defective starter switch (Courtesy U.S. Coast Guard—CG 151)

—Other common electrical problems that often can be corrected without great difficulty are fouled spark plugs and faulty breaker points (in a mechanical ignition system). The points are inside the distributor and may be examined by removing the distributor cap (see illustration).

—See that the breaker points are opening and closing as the engine is cranked. When wide open the gap should measure about .02 inches (exact gap can be obtained from engine manual). Turning the adjusting screw allows proper gap setting, which should be measured with a feeler gauge or perhaps a matchbook cover in an emergency. If points are corroded or pitted, dress them with a fine file (a fingernail file will do). Put a drop of light oil on the breaker arm pivot.

—The rotor lies under the distributor cap. Both the cap, including its terminals, and the rotor arm should be dry and clean. It often helps to spray them with WD-40 or CRC.

—Spark plugs can become fouled from carbon or oil. They can be cleaned with a fine file, sandpaper, and a degreaser. The plug gap should be set to a width specified by the engine manual; otherwise try .035 inches (a shade less than the thickness of two matchbook covers). Replace damaged plugs (such as those showing signs of serious overheating). Always carry spares.

—Another form of spark plug fouling is from moisture (water) sometimes occuring after heavy weather. Remove high tension wires to plugs by first twisting slightly before lifting them up by their boots. Remove plugs, blow on them, and dry off with a towel. Saturated plugs may need to be dried close to a flame to boil out the water, and you might need to turn over the engine with the plugs out to remove any water from the cylinders.

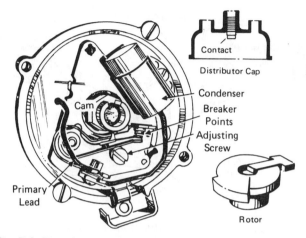

Fig. 7-6. Distributor with cap removed (Courtesy U.S. Coast Guard—CG 151)

—Ignition diagnosis is often performed with spark tests: Remove a spark plug cable from its plug, hold its exposed terminal a quarter inch from the engine block (to ground), crank the engine, and observe whether or not a healthy spark is produced. A spark indicates carburation problems and/or fouled plugs. If there is no spark, a similar spark test should be made with the secondary (large) high tension wire from the distributor cap to the coil (see illustration). *Warning:* The coil converts low voltage current to high voltage that can produce a powerful shock, so don't hold high tension cables by hand; you can use insulated pliers. *Warning*: be sure there are no gas fumes when spark tests are performed (see Chapter 4). A healthy spark indicates trouble in the distributor or spark plug wires. Try drying and spraying the distributor cap and rotor with WD-40 or CRC.

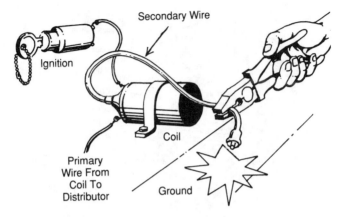

Fig. 7-7. Spark testing secondary high tension wire from coil to distributor (Courtesy U.S. Coast Guard—CG 151)

—Spark plugs can also become wet with gasoline (smell them). This indicates flooding (perhaps from excessive choking). The engine might be started after waiting several minutes or after removing excess gas by cranking the engine with throttle and choke wide open.

—If spark plugs are completely dry (no gas reaching them), check the air vent on the gas tank to see that it is not clogged.

—Fuel starvation may also be caused by clogged jets in the carborator or a stuck fuel pump. Some gentle taps on the bodies of the pump or carborator with a hammer may temporarily cure the problem (tapping may also loosen a stuck Bendix pinion on a starting motor).

—Spare belts should be carried, but if not, one might be fashioned from a piece of line. Tie the line with a sheet bend and tighten it by adjusting the movable pulley.

STEERING FAILURE

—The most frequent causes of steering failure are broken cables or links between a steering wheel and the rudder quadrant, a broken rudder head fitting (where a tiller joins the rudder stock or post), and a bent or broken spade rudder stock (see Chapter 1). These parts should be examined periodically.

—See that no strands in the steering cable are broken; that the cable sheaves are secure (preferably bolted), properly aligned, and turn freely; and that there is no slack in the cable.

—Rudder head fittings come in a variety of types. Check for cracks, wear, or looseness of bolts or keys.

—With spade rudders check for wear, cracks, corrosion, binding, and straightness of the stock. When the boat is hauled have someone hold the tiller while you apply pres-

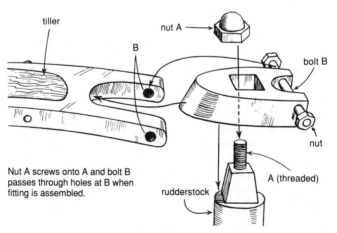

Nut A screws onto A and bolt B passes through holes at B when fitting is assembled.

Fig. 7-8. Rudder head fitting

sure to the rudder blade to check for play, wobble, or looseness.

— With other types of rudders examine the pintles (pins), gudgeons (pin eyes), and heel fittings (at the bottom of the blade) for security, corrosion, and wear.

— Although tillers seldom break without warning, look for any signs of cracking or delamination and check the resistance to bending.

— Every cruising boat with a wheel should carry an emergency tiller that will fit over the head of the rudder stock. When the wheel is just forward of the stock, the emergency tiller might be a bent pipe that curves over the top of the wheel, or else the tiller might be rigged backwards and steered like a wheel (push it in the direction you want to go).

— Long distance cruisers should carry a jury (emergency) rudder or materials from which a jury rudder can be made. On my 37-foot sloop, I use the plywood engine compartment door for the jury rudder blade, which is almost exactly the size of the primary rudder. This is bolted to a bent steel rod (the jury stock) which turns inside a pipe that is fastened with hose clamps to the stern pulpit (see illustration). A steering yoke is welded to the top of the stock.

— Other emergency steering alternatives are: a stern sweep (long oar lashed to the stern), which might be made from a boom or pole with a piece of wood fastened to its overboard end to serve as a blade; a drag towed astern, which can be shifted from side to side; steering by varying the speed of twin screws; or steering with sails. Of course, a self steering vane that has an oar (its own rudder) can be used if the boat is so equipped.

— Shifting a drag from one side of the stern to the other can be accomplished by tying steering lines with rolling

Fig. 7-9. Emergency tiller (rigged backwards)

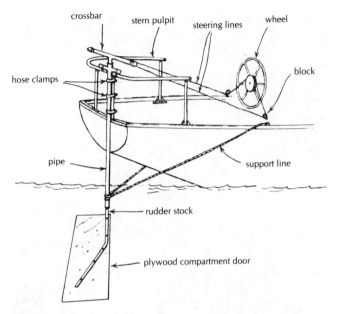

Fig. 7-10. Offshore jury rudder on the author's boat

hitches to the drag's towline (see illustration). The drag
might be a tire, bucket, milk crate, or small drogue (see
Chapter 8). The effectiveness of this system can be improved with a spar (spinnaker pole perhaps) lashed across
the afterdeck as illustrated to extend outboard the leads
for the steering lines.

—Whether or not a boat can be steered successfully with
sails depends on her balance. She should have a slight lee
helm (see Chapter 2) when sailing in moderate winds under jib alone. When this is the case, the boat can be made
to bear off by trimming forward sails and slacking after
sails. Of course, the opposite is done when you wish to
head up.

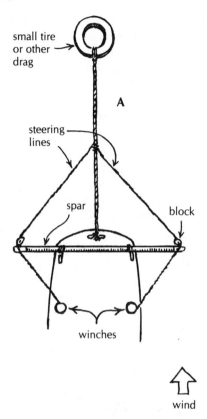

small tire
or other
drag

A

steering
lines

spar

block

winches

wind

Fig. 7-11. Jury steering by shifting a drag

RIGGING FAILURE

Sound rigging practices to avoid failure were discussed in Chapter 2. To reiterate the key points: be sure that your standing rigging is in straight alignment and well toggled to prevent metal fatigue; that potentially vulnerable areas of the rigging such as swages, pins, tangs, and spreader fittings are periodically examined for cracks or security; that there is no evidence of chafe; and that the rigging is tuned to prevent undue bending of the mast. Replace rigging when it is badly chafed or when wire strands have broken. In the event of a rigging problem or failure take the following emergency actions promptly:

—Luff up at once and tack if a windward shroud breaks while sailing close hauled. Bear off if the windward shroud breaks while you are broad reaching. The shroud will usually break at the lower swage or just above it. Repair by bending the broken wire around a large thimble and fastening it to the stand part with bulldog clips. (You may need to use a Norseman or preferably a Sta-Lok terminal for 1 × 19 wire with a diameter greater than ¼ inch.) The resulting eye can be connected to the chainplates with shackles or a short length of chain.

—Bear off at once and run before the wind if a jibstay should happen to break. Keep the jib hoisted until spare halyards can be run forward, secured to the stemhead, and then winched taut.

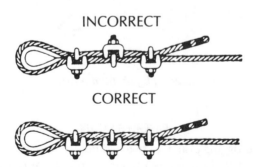

Fig. 7-12. Bulldog clips used correctly and incorrectly (From Handbook for Riggers *by W. G. Newberry)*

— Head up promptly and trim in the mainsail flat if the backstay breaks. Lower headsails and use topping lift and mainsheet (with mainsail lowered) to pull the masthead aft. Set up running backstays if you have them. Broken backstays are usually caused by over-tensioning the stays with hydraulic adjusters or the shock loading of spinnakers repeatedly collapsing and suddenly filling.

— Get in the habit of observing. For example, check your spreaders before tacking to see that they have not escaped their sockets or slipped on their shrouds. With a quick glance, check that no shrouds are hanging free.

— Compensation for a broken spreader can be achieved with a spinnaker pole set at the bottom of its track (close to the deck) at right angles to the boat's centerline. The broken spreader's shroud can be run through and lashed to the outboard end of the pole and attached to the chainplate with a length of chain or wire strap. If the spreader holds the shroud away from the mast at an angle of 10 degrees, a spinnaker pole three times longer than the spreader set at twice the distance from masthead to the spreader would produce a healthy angle of about 15 degrees. Be sure to rig guys from the pole to hold it steady.

— See that the angles between the top of a spreader and its shroud and the bottom of the spreader and its shroud are equal (see Chapter 2). A spreader tip that has slipped on its shroud can be lifted or at least supported by shackling a halyard to the shroud and hauling the shackle aloft where it will bear against the spreader tip.

— Masts can be broken by pumping in a seaway. To help steady the mast, set up on running backstays and, if you don't have these, run halyards under the spreaders and secure them aft. This will help hold the middle of the mast steady. In severe conditions when the pumping cannot be controlled, slow down or try sailing a different course.

—Broken spars can be repaired temporarily by fishing, i.e., lashing, taping, or screwing splints on both sides of the break.

—If the mast should happen to go by the board (fall overboard), check the welfare of your crew and then immediately check to see that the mast is not pounding against the hull. When there is a danger of the hull being holed, the spar may have to be detached from the vessel. This is most easily done by removing the rigging pins, but every offshore boat should carry heavy duty cable cutters. Bronze cotter pins are more easily removed than those of stainless steel.

—Restepping a mast or raising a section of a broken spar to serve as jury mast can be done with a gin pole as illustrated or else with an A-frame (an inverted V made from two spars fastened together at the top). Sometimes the main boom can be used for a gin pole. The mast heel must be securely lashed to prevent it from sliding forward when the mast is first lifted.

—Jury rigs can be fashioned from spars such as booms and spinnaker poles well supported with numerous rope or wire shrouds and stays. Short vertical spars can carry small sails or larger sails reefed and/or hoisted by the foot. Sometimes a large sail can have its head knotted to reduce its size. Canadian singlehander John Hughes sailed his 41-foot sloop 4,400 miles, including a rounding of the notorious Cape Horn, under a jury rig consisting of tiny sails supported by an A-frame made from two spinnaker poles with their lower ends planted in rag-filled coffee cans.

—The greatest enemy of the offshore sailor is chafe. Constantly check lines to see that they are not being rubbed. Use chafe guards such as plastic or rubber hoses at points of wear, and tie off or fairlead lines that are being chafed.

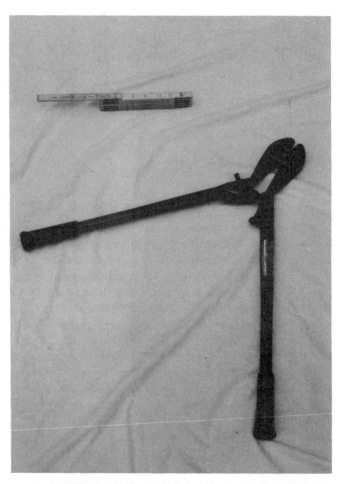

Fig. 7-13. Rigging cutters

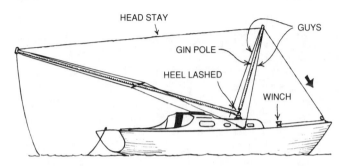

Fig. 7-14. Restepping a mast

COLLISIONS AND SERIOUS LEAKS

— In the event of a collision check the welfare of your crew and then the condition of the boat. If the collision has been with another boat and the two vessels are stuck together, make a thorough inspection of both boats before separation. It may be necessary to render assistance or remove crew from the more damaged to the less damaged vessel. Identifications must be exchanged between boats and, later, accident reports must be filed if there is serious injury or damage. An injury is considered serious if it requires medical assistance beyond first aid. Property damage is serious when the repair is more than $500, although some state laws require a report when the damage exceeds $200. Reports are filed with a designated state office (such as the Department of Natural Resources) or the Coast Guard.

— A stove-in hull resulting from a collision with flotsam or some other object might be temporarily repaired by stuffing pillows or clothing into the hole, covering the packing with plywood, and applying shores (poles or props) that can be wedged against the plywood to hold it in place.

Offshore boats should carry a small sheet or two of plywood and items such as oars or spars that can be used for shores.

— A collision mat (see Chapter 1) should be a part of the damage control kit on every long-distance, offshore vessel. Whatever the shape of the mat (some are square or triangular and others are octagonal), there should be plenty of grommets to which lashing lines can be secured. When water flow through a hole cannot be stopped from inside the hull, the hole should be covered with a collision mat on the hull's exterior where water pressure (together with the lashing lines) will hold the mat in place. The mat or smaller piece of cloth might also be held in place with underwater epoxy such as Devcon UW.

— Carry a diagram that shows all plumbing, piping, and valves (see illustration).

— After a holing from a collision with flotsam (or something else), slow down at once, locate the leak, and tack to attempt lifting the hole above water. Even if the hole is still immersed, the water flow can be slowed by lifting the hole closer to the surface. It has been said, for example, that a 1½-inch diameter hole admits 25 gallons per minute less at 2 feet than at 4 feet below the surface.

— When underway, the bilge should be checked periodically. On offshore boats, it is common practice to inspect the bilge when the watch is changed, but if the boat is making water, the inspection obviously should be more often.

— In the event of an unexplainable leak, slow down and then immediately check all through-hull fittings, such as seacocks and their hoses, knotmeter sensors, and stuffing boxes for the propeller shaft and rudder stock. Faults can be temporarily remedied by closing the valves, driving tapered wooden plugs into the holes (see Chapter 1), or by

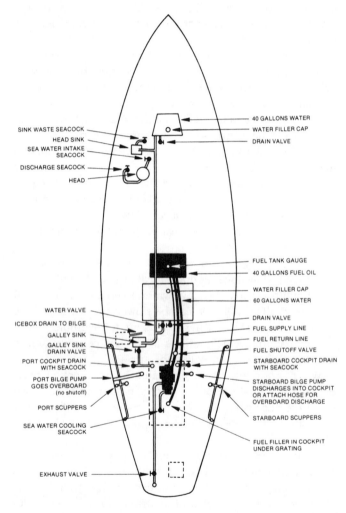

SINK WASTE SEACOCK
HEAD SINK
SEA WATER INTAKE SEACOCK
DISCHARGE SEACOCK
HEAD

40 GALLONS WATER
WATER FILLER CAP
DRAIN VALVE

FUEL TANK GAUGE
40 GALLONS FUEL OIL
WATER FILLER CAP
60 GALLONS WATER

WATER VALVE
ICEBOX DRAIN TO BILGE
GALLEY SINK
GALLEY SINK DRAIN VALVE
PORT COCKPIT DRAIN WITH SEACOCK
PORT BILGE PUMP GOES OVERBOARD (no shutoff)
PORT SCUPPERS
SEA WATER COOLING SEACOCK

DRAIN VALVE
FUEL SUPPLY LINE
FUEL RETURN LINE
FUEL SHUTOFF VALVE
STARBOARD COCKPIT DRAIN WITH SEACOCK
STARBOARD BILGE PUMP DISCHARGES INTO COCKPIT OR ATTACH HOSE FOR OVERBOARD DISCHARGE
STARBOARD SCUPPERS
FUEL FILLER IN COCKPIT UNDER GRATING

EXHAUST VALVE

Fig. 7-15. Piping diagram (From Sail and Power *by Richard Henderson)*

setting up on the packing nuts of stuffing boxes. Still another source of flooding is from the back-siphoning of a bilge pump. See that the discharge line is looped high above the waterline, and if possible, that it has an antisiphon vent.

— Wherever possible, see that hoses are attached with two hose clamps and periodically inspect to see that the clamps are tight. Exercise your seacocks and especially gate valves, which can freeze up if never used.

— Leaks from open seams can be stemmed with caulking cotton and a mixture of cup grease and putty or perhaps underwater epoxy.

— To cope with flooding or serious leaks, be sure there are adequate bailers. An offshore boat needs at least one high capacity bilge pump below and one on deck, operable from the helm, plus a portable bilge pump and several buckets. One trick to clear a flooded bilge quickly is to shut off the seacock for the engine's seawater intake, place the hose (with a strainer on its end) in the bilge, and then start the engine. Be sure to stop the engine when the bilge water has been removed. It is a good idea to add a bilge suction hose to the intake hose connecting it with a T-fitting and valve, in order to avoid the need for detaching the intake.

FIRE

The most common sources of fire are from stove and engine fuels, especially gasoline (safe fueling practices were discussed in Chapter 4). Liquified petroleum (LP) gas, such as propane and butane, used to fuel galley stoves, should be given the same respect as gasoline, for it is highly explosive and, being heavier than air, can sink into the bilge. Fire extinguishers were briefly discussed in

Chapter 1, but here are some tips on preventing fires and further advice on fighting them:

— Be sure that the fuel system is properly grounded to prevent sparks from static electricity.

— Especially with a gasoline engine, continually check for leaks in the fuel system and sniff for fumes.

— Parts of the engine exhaust system that are not water-cooled need insulation.

— Use non-spark switches (no knife-blade types) and be sure that all electric wiring is fused or fitted with circuit breakers.

— Be sure there are no towels or curtains hung above or close to the galley stove.

— See that bulkhead heating stoves are well insulated and fitted with tile bases.

— See that there are fire extinguishers available to the galley and the engine compartment areas. Check and maintain your extinguishers.

— Be sure that fuel shut-off valves are sufficiently far from stoves that they can be reached without exposing hands and arms to flames in the event of a stove fire.

— See that all flexible fuel lines in areas that could be exposed to flames are fireproof and that through-hull plumbing hoses in the engine compartment are at least highly fire resistant.

— Never leave a cooking stove unwatched, especially when there is a breeze that could blow out the flame. An extinguished burner left open is particularly dangerous when another burner is lit.

— Never light an alcohol pressure stove without having a pot or kettle of water handy. Water will extinguish an alcohol flare-up, but be sure to use enough water to prevent smoldering and possible reignition.

Fig. 7-16. Fire can spread rapidly after an explosion of gasoline fumes in an open bilge.

— LP gas cylinders should be kept in deck lockers that are vented overboard. Cylinder valves should be kept closed and only turned on before stoves are used. Be sure the stove valves are closed when a cylinder valve is opened. When you are through using the stove, close the cylinder valves first to assure that no fuel remains in the line.

—To avoid the risk of fire from spontaneous combustion see that lockers are well ventilated and don't keep soiled rags used for cleaning up oil or paint. Avoid stowage of any highly flammable materials.

—See that coal or wood burning stoves have proper stacks to prevent backdrafts and spark emissions.

—Be sure your batteries are properly ventilated with holes at the top of the battery box to vent explosive hydrogen gas.

—With class-A fires use water (easily obtained with a draw bucket). Shut off fuel supply at once with a class-B fire, and switch off electricity with class-C fires (fire classification was given in Chapter 1).

—Slow down and change heading of a burning boat to reduce apparent wind and direct the flames away from the most flammable areas.

—If the fire is out of control call for help before the fire reaches your radio or you are forced to shut down power.

—Learn how to operate your fire extinguisher (instructions are normally on the extinguisher). The extinguishing agent is directed at the base of the flames. Don't use water on an electrical fire unless the electricity is turned off.

—A fire can be extinguished by reduction or elimination of heat, fuel, and oxygen. Water can be used to cool areas that might ignite. Fuel is reduced not only by closing fuel valves, but also by throwing burning or smoldering objects overboard.

— If possible, deprive the fire of oxygen by keeping hatches and doors closed and/or smothering the fire. A wet towel can often be used effectively to smother a galley fire.

— Avoid breathing Halon, especially Halon 104 and 1211, for prolonged periods in an enclosed compartment. The same warning should be given for carbon dioxide (CO_2), as it is an oxygen-depriving gas, which is sufficiently depleting to stop a running engine.

— Wear protective clothing such as foul weather gear when fighting a fire.

— Act at once when there is a fire, as any delay in fighting it allows the temperature to rise and makes extinguishing much more difficult, if not impossible.

— Keep yourself low when fighting a fire in a smoke-filled compartment.

— Periodically check your extinguishers. Occasionally shake a dry chemical extinguisher to prevent the contents from hardening and, of course, check the pressure gauge.

CREW OVERBOARD

Common causes for crew falling overboard are:

— Carelessness and haste in moving about the boat in rough waters. Heed the expression "one hand for the ship."

— Failure to wear and use safety harnesses.

— Inadequate lifelines, pulpits, and grab rails.

— Ineffective skidproofing of slippery decks. Unless the decks are raw teak, they need a molded-in rough textured surface, glued-on skidproof pads, or nonslip paints.

— Failure to rig a jibing preventer (a line or tackle holding the boom forward) when running before the wind.

— Leaving loose, unfurled sails on the foredeck.

— Failure to wear proper, nonskid deck shoes.

— Relieving one's bladder over the side rather than using the head.

— Sudden turning or acceleration in a fast motorboat.

— Standing up while pulling the starter rope of an outboard motor.

— Sitting on the gunwale, foredeck, or afterdeck of a high-speed boat.

— The parting of a lifeline or its attachment. Inspect lifelines periodically and renew lashings when they look suspicious.

The following actions are helpful in recovering a crew member who should happen to go overboard:

— Shout "man overboard to port (or starboard)" to alert other crew.

— If under power, swing the stern away from the victim to assure he or she will not be cut by the propeller.

— Immediately throw overboard a life preserver such as a ring buoy or floating cushion as close as possible to the victim. This is vital when the victim is not wearing a personal flotation device (PFD).

— Slow down and stay close to the victim to assure that he or she can be kept in sight.

— One crew member should continually keep his or her eyes on the victim and point to the victim's location.

— On most points of sailing, in a small sailboat in fair weather with moderate winds, the fastest and most efficient method of returning to the victim is with a moderately quick jibe, which will bring the boat with headway lost (sail flapping) rapidly and directly to the person overboard. This maneuver will put you sufficiently far to leeward that you can slow down when making the pickup.

— In heavier weather and on larger boats with complicated gear the quick-stop method is often preferred. With this method, the boat is immediately luffed head-to-wind, then tacked and temporarily hove-to with jib aback (see Chapter 8). The boat is then headed off to a run and the jib is lowered. When the victim is abaft the beam, the boat is jibed and luffed up alongside (see illustration). Another alternative when shorthanded is to allow the hove-to boat to drift down on the victim when the boat is directly upwind of him or her.

—A commonly used device for shorthanded rescues is the Lifesling, a horsecollar type of buoy trailed behind the boat at the end of a long floating line. The boat circles the victim until he or she can grab the line and enter the sling (put it under the arms). When not in use, the sling is normally carried in a yellow pouch attached to the stern pulpit. Illustrated instructions are printed on the pouch (see photo).

— If the victim is not seen falling overboard and cannot be seen in the water, the helmsman should note the compass course as soon as it is realized that a crew member is missing. Then the boat should be turned (downwind in fair weather) and headed onto a reciprocal course (180 degrees from the original course) to begin a slow careful search along the boat's original track.

— Even on a smart performing, highly maneuverable sailboat, engines can be helpful in returning and maneuvering to pick up a victim, but great care must be taken to prevent lines from fouling the propeller and to avoid cutting the victim with the prop.

—When coming alongside the person overboard in a boat under sail, it is usually best to stop with sails luffing just to windward of the victim so that the boat forms a lee and drifts towards rather than away from the victim. Even if the jib is lowered it often pays to keep the mainsail hoisted to help prevent the boat from rolling when beam-to the seas.

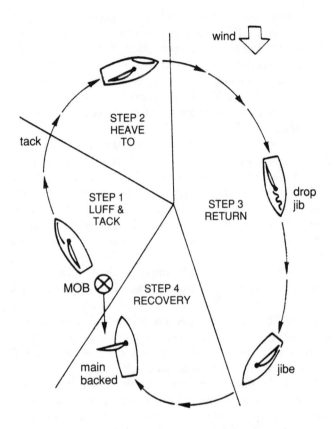

Fig. 7-17. Person overboard recovery, quick-stop method (From Sail and Power *by Richard Henderson)*

—Under power it may be better to maneuver to leeward of the victim to assure that he or she will not be cut by the prop.

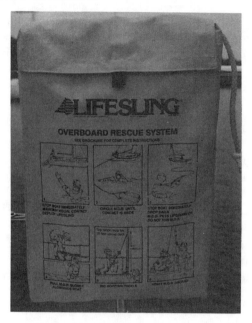

Fig. 7-18. Pouch containing Lifesling and tether

—When close to the victim, throw a heaving line that will float to him or her. Secure the victim to the boat while devising a method of lifting the person aboard.

—When victims are not injured or exhausted, they can be helped aboard with ladders, such as a fold-down stern ladder or Jacob's ladder (a type used by pilots boarding ships), a scramble net, or halyard on a winch. When using a stern ladder, keep the boat beam-to the seas, so that she will roll rather than pitch and possibly "bean" the victim with her counter.

—Injured or exhausted victims can be brought aboard with a tackle rigged from a spar such as the mainboom, the main halyard, or possibly a davit (for lifting an anchor or tender) on a large boat. When extra power is needed, the tackle's fall (hauling part) can be led to a powerful sheet winch. Head boat into the seas when the victim is lifted over the side.

EMERGENCY COMMUNICATIONS

Distress Signals

The following signals, used or exhibited together or separately, indicate distress and need of assistance. Except for the last two signals, the signal list below is taken from Rule 37 of the International Rules of the Road.

—A gun or other explosive signal fired at intervals of about a minute.

—A continuous sounding with any fog-signaling apparatus.

—Rockets or shells, throwing red stars fired one at a time at short intervals

—A signal made by radiotelegraphy or by any other signaling method consisting of the group $\cdots---\cdots$ (SOS) in the Morse code.

—A signal sent by radiotelephony consisting of the spoken word "Mayday."

—The International Code Signal of distress indicated by NC.

—A signal consisting of a square flag having above or below it a ball or anything resembling a ball.

—Flames on the vessel (as from a burning tar barrel, oil barrel, etc.)

—A rocket parachute flare or a hand flare showing a red light.

—A smoke signal giving off orange-colored smoke.

— Slowly and repeatedly raising and lowering arms out-stretched to each side.

— The radiotelegraph alarm signal.

— The radiotelephone alarm signal.

— Signals transmitted by emergency position-indicating radio beacons (EPIRBS).

— A piece of orange-colored canvas with either a black square and circle or other appropriate symbol (for identification from the air).

— Dye marker (any color).

— A high intensity white light flashing at regular intervals from 50 to 70 times per minute (a strobe light [in Rule 37 of the Inland Rules]).

— National flag or ensign hoisted upside down. (Although not listed in the Rules of the Road, this signal is almost universally recognized).

Radio Transmissions

Even though many sailors prefer to "get away from the telephone" when they go boating, a radiophone does increase safety by providing a means of calling for help in the event of an emergency. If a permanent radiophone is not installed, a cruiser should carry an EPIRB (see Chapter 1), or for short range communications, perhaps a portable VHF (very high frequency) transmitter; or a portable radiophone that transmits voice on the MF (medium frequency) international distress frequency 2182 KHz; or CB (citizens band) 27 MHz portable radio (channel 9 is used for emergencies); or a UHF (ultrahigh frequency) 800 MHz cellular phone. Of course, portable equipment can be carried in a life raft or dinghy in the event it is necessary to abandon ship.

— Class A and B EPIRBs transmit alarm signals on the aviation emergency frequencies 121.5 and 243 MHz. Class

Fig. 7-19. EPIRBs carried offshore on the author's boat

C EPIRBS send out alarms on VHF channels 15 and 16, while the 406 EPIRB (operating on 406 MHz) activates SAR (search and rescue) satellites. The latter is long-range and most suitable for long-distance, offshore voyaging. It should be registered with the National Oceanographic and Atmospheric Administration (NOAA) (a registration card is included with the purchase of an EPIRB).

—VHF, operating in the bands between 156 and 162 MHz, is about the simplest form of reliable marine communication, but its range is limited to little more than line of sight (perhaps 10 to 30 or more miles) depending on the power of the set and heights of the sending and receiving antennas. The Coast Guard uses the following formula to determine VHF range: $1.4 \sqrt{Hboat} + 1.4 \sqrt{HCG}$, where H is antenna height (for boat and CG station).

—When long distance communication is needed, the VHF can be supplemented (not replaced) with a SSB (single sideband) radio operating on the MF and HF (high frequency) bands (typically, 8 through 25 MHz frequencies). This is a relatively expensive and power-hungry radio that needs good grounding and a long antenna (normally the backstay of a cruising sailboat). Performance is very much affected by atmospheric and sunspot activity. As a general rule, it is best to use for transmission the frequency that you can most clearly receive.

—Amateur (ham) radio, which has a tremendous spread of frequencies, is another way to communicate over long distances. The drawbacks are stringent licensing requirements (the operator must know Morse code), and there is no specific distress channel, although help can almost always be obtained from cooperative hams on shore or on other boats.

—Distress, urgency, and safety frequencies, which should be monitored whenever the radio is on, are channel 16

(156.8 MHz) for VHF and 2182 KHz for medium frequency. When non-emergency calls are made, parties can be contacted on these frequencies initially, but then the calls must be transferred to working channels. The Coast Guard maintains three-minute silent periods immediately after the hour and half-hour on 2182 KHz. Only distress or urgency calls are made during the silent periods.

— Distress calls, using the spoken word MAYDAY (m'aidez, French for help me), have priority over any other message. A call is begun with a radiophone warbling alarm signal (if available), followed by MAYDAY (spoken three times), followed by THIS IS (spoken once), followed by the name of the vessel in distress (spoken three times) and the once-spoken call sign (assigned by the Federal Communications Commission).

After this, the distress message is given:

1) MAYDAY (spoken once).
2) Name of vessel (spoken once).
3) Position of vessel (perhaps the distance and bearing from an aid to navigation).
4) Nature of distress (sinking, fire, etc.).
5) Kind of assistance needed (pumps, doctor, etc.).
6) Information to facilitate rescue (description of vessel in distress—number of crew).
7) The word OVER, meaning temporarily ending transmission. The word OUT permanently ends the transmission.

— Urgency calls are made for less imminently dangerous situations such as the vessel or crew in jeopardy or any case where you don't need immediate help. The alarm signal is the spoken word PAN-PAN (pronounced PAHN-PAHN) repeated twice. (Pan comes from a French word meaning breakdown.)

A (WHITE & BLUE)
I have a diver down; keep
well clear at slow speed.

(Also, a red square flag with a diagonal
white stripe warns that a diver is down.)

 K (YELLOW & BLUE)
I wish to communicate
with you.

 B (RED)
I am taking in or discharging
or carrying dangerous goods.

(Also the protest flag for racing yachts.)

 N (BLUE & WHITE)
No (negative).

 C (BLUE & WHITE WITH
RED MIDDLE STRIPE)
Yes (affirmative).

 O (YELLOW & RED)
Man overboard.

 D (BLUE & YELLOW)
Keep clear of me; I am
maneuvering with difficulty.

 U (RED & WHITE)
You are running into
danger.

 F (WHITE & RED)
I am disabled.
Communicate with me.

 V (RED & WHITE)
I require assistance.

 G (YELLOW & BLUE)
I require a pilot.

 W (BLUE & WHITE WITH
RED CENTER)
I require medical assistance.

SPECIAL CLUB SIGNALS (should be flown under club burgee so as
not to be confused with International Code)

 T

(RED, WHITE & BLUE)

Tender needed. Send club launch.
(Under # 102: Keep clear of me,
I am engaged in pair trawling.)

 Q

(YELLOW)

Come within hail.
(Under # 102: My vessel
is healthy and I request
free pratique.)

Fig. 7-20. Important single flag signals from International
Code of Signals, *DMAHTC Publication 102*

— Safety calls are for lower priority situations such as meteorological warnings or potentially dangerous flotsam. These calls are also made on channel 16 or 2182 KHz, but together with a request to shift to a working frequency where the safety message will be given. The safety call alarm is the spoken word SECURITY (pronounced SAY-CURITAY) repeated twice.

Flag Signals

Not all boats have transmitting radios, of course, and those that have them may be subject to lack of common frequency or possible radio failure (from loss of power, a lightning strike, damaged antenna, corrosion, water saturation, etc.). It is therefore prudent for a cruiser to carry a bag of signal flags. Single flag signals are a useful means of conveying a simple urgent or important message to another boat or a nearby shore. The accompanying illustration shows some of the more important single flag signals from the DMAHTC (Defense Mapping Agency Hydrographic/Topographic Center) Publication 102. The bottom two flag signals are not from this publication, but they are commonly recognized yacht club signals. So as not to be confused with International Code signals, they should be hoisted just beneath a yacht club burgee. The transmitting station should always hoist a signal where it is most easily seen. Usually this will be beneath the mainmast spreaders or yardarm.

8. Heavy Weather

If I were asked for advice by a young shipmaster I should say, 'When possible—and I know it is not always possible—stay at least 250 miles from the center of a major storm, or at least clear of the confused seas, in order that you may escape.

But whatever decision you may make, if you get into trouble, you may be sure that someone, who was not there, will come up with something you should have done. —Lt. Cdr. A.G. Graham, USNR (Ret.).

There are many theories about the best way to handle heavy weather, but no one should be dogmatic about storm tactics because of such variables as the behavioral differences of various types of vessels, variations in weather and current, bottom and shore effects, and the unpredictable nature of ocean waves. What might work well for one boat in a certain set of circumstances might not work for a different boat or a similar boat in other conditions. However, every seaman should be aware of general principles of weather, sea, and boat behavior and be aware of the tactical options.

WEATHER BASICS

Not much detail on the general subject of weather will be given here, as most readers are familiar with the basics from exposure to constant weather reports on television or in the newspapers (further information can be found in the Cornell Boaters Library book called *The Boater's Weather Guide* by Margaret Williams). Here are some of the more important basics of weather in abbreviated form:

— Highs (anticyclones) are atmospheric high pressure mounds about which the wind circles in an outward direction. The Coriolis force (a deflecting force caused by the earth's rotation) makes the wind rotate in a clockwise direction around a high in the northern hemisphere (counterclockwise in the southern hemisphere). Good weather is normally associated with highs.

— Lows (cyclones) are atmospheric sinkholes of low pressure around which the wind circles in an inward direction (toward the low's center). In the northern hemisphere the wind rotates around the low counterclockwise (clockwise in the southern hemisphere). Bad weather is almost always associated with a low.

— Winds tend to flow from a high into a low. Sometimes there is a "gearwheeling" effect that increases the wind velocity between a high and a low. When two highs and two lows are arranged so that their winds are opposed, there will usually be a calm area in the middle known as a col. Winds are also usually calm or light at the center of a high.

— In very general terms, the winds aloft, including jet streams or steering currents that guide the movement of surface weather, move from west to east in the middle latitudes (from about 60 to 30 degrees). Easterly trade winds prevail between about 30 degrees and close to the equator. At the boundary between westerlies and easterlies the wind is usually variable.

— The westerly flow is interrupted or deviated by lows, highs (which often slow or block the weather movement), sea breezes (suction wind from the water to hot land), and other phenomena. One deviating influence over the United States is an occasional low-level jet stream east of the Rocky Mountains which provides a southerly component to the weather movement. This is reinforced on the East Coast by wind circulation around the Bermuda High (an Atlantic high near Bermuda frequently occuring during the summer). Weather often moves up the Atlantic coast rather than proceeding directly offshore.

—Fronts are boundaries between warm and cold air masses. An advancing front pushed by cold air is a cold front and a front pushed by warm air is a warm front. If there is no movement, of course, the front is stationary. A cold front will often overtake a slower moving warm front, and this produces an occluded front with the probability of foul if not severe weather.

—Fog is formed when water vapor in the air cools and condenses into suspended water droplets that block visibility. The most troublesome kind of fog for offshore boaters is advection fog, which is formed when warm air passes over cool waters. Particularly troublesome areas of the United States are Maine when summer southerly winds blow over cold water carried south by the Labrador current, and northern California when warm ocean winds blow over coastal waters that are cooled by upwelling (water rising from the bottom). The best weather broadcasts often provide the dew point (temperature at which condensation occurs) and if you have a thermometer you will have a clue as to whether or not fog is likely. A considerable and continuing spread between the air temperature and dew point indicates that fog is not apt to occur. In foggy regions, a few boats carry psychrometers, which are instruments that determine relative humidity and dew point.

TYPES OF STORMS

Typical kinds of heavy weather affecting boaters during the boating season are thunderstorms, twisters, microbursts, extratropical lows, weather bombs (on rare occasions), hurricanes, and anticyclonic gales.

—Thunderstorms are caused by the lifting of moist, unstable air. There are two principle types affecting the boater: air-mass and frontal storms. The former is a local squall usually caused by the heating of land in the late afternoon on a humid summer day in coastal or inland waters. This type often can be anticipated when, on such a day, there is significant vertical development of cumulus clouds (low-level, puffy clouds) to the west in middle latitudes. When a cloud towers up to 25,000 feet or more and has turned dark at its base, it has developed into a mature cumulonimbus cloud (a thunderhead). In the dissipating stage its top flares out like an anvil. Frontal thunderstorms form along a front or ahead of it in the form of a squall line (a row of storms). Because warm air is thrown aloft so rapidly by a fast moving cold front this kind of front can produce the most violent type of thunderstorm.

—Twisters are mini-tornadoes. A full-fledged tornado, which can be devastating over land (with winds that can exceed 300 m.p.h. and low pressure that can cause buildings to explode) is seldom as violent over water. Offshore it will be mollified by the water and will normally turn into a waterspout. Concentrated into a very small area of spinning wind, twisters may only hit you momentarily, but they can cause severe knockdowns and even lift a towed dinghy to the end of her painter. Tornadoes are produced along fronts and squall lines when cold air meets extremely warm, moist air. A warning sign is mammatus (breast-shaped) development on the underside of a cumulonimbus cloud.

—Microbursts are the opposite of tornadoes in that they produce very powerful downdrafts rather than updrafts. They most often develop during overcast, unsettled weather and are associated with fronts and thunderheads; however, they can occur as "white squalls" in clear weather when cold air aloft suddenly drops to the surface. Perhaps one in a hundred or more thunderstorms will produce a microburst that can seriously endanger an airplane or boat. Sailboats are vulnerable not only to a powerful initial gust but also to a severe wind shift when the outflow from the downburst fans out after striking the

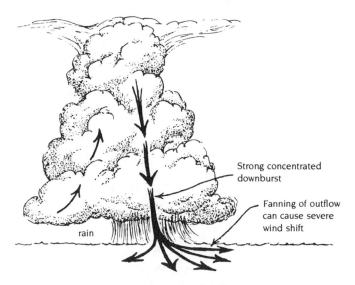

Fig. 8-1. Microburst emanating within a thunderstorm

water surface. At least five tall ships (with relatively low stability ranges and slow methods of reducing sail) have been sunk by microbursts.

— Extratropical lows are cyclones that originate outside of the tropics. They usually form along fronts or to leeward of prominent mountain ranges and produce broad areas of rainy, stormy weather. The accompanying illustration shows the development of a typical extratropical low as it moves across the United States. Note that it starts with a crested wave in the front where the pressure is low. A rapid moving cold front forms to the left of the low, and it gradually overtakes the warm front on the right of the low. When the tail of the cold front hits the warm Gulf Stream (a prominent current) off the East Coast, it will sometimes form a secondary low. There is usually a long period of advanced warning preceding the warm front with high altitude clouds, then lower clouds filling the sky, and a falling barometer. A cold front approaches more rapidly with the more sudden appearance of clouds (usually cumulonimbus in unstable air).

— Weather bombs are severe extratropical lows that deepen with almost explosive rapidity. They most often form near or in the Gulf Stream or the Kuroshio current in the Pacific and are most common in the winter. A notorious summer bomb was the devastating Fastnet storm in 1979 that caused the abandonment of twenty-four racing yachts and the loss of fifteen lives. The forecasting of that bomb, a secondary low, was made more difficult by a Fujiwhara effect (the rotating of two lows about a point between them).

— Hurricanes, called typhoons in some parts of the world, are severe cyclones that originate in the tropics. They differ from extratropical lows in that they have warm cores, and they are much more symmetrical, with the strongest winds revolving around a relatively small, calm center

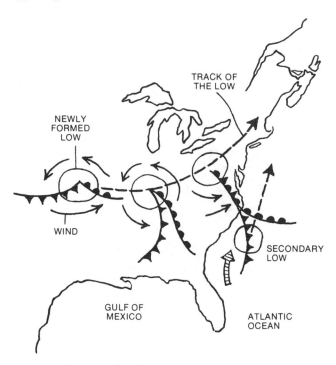

Fig. 8-2. Development of an extratropical low and secondary low. See key on page 231.

called the eye. Hurricanes are generally much more severe than extratropical lows, but the latter can, on rare occasions, have winds of hurricane strength. In most tropical oceans tropical cyclones are seasonal, beginning in early summer and peaking in the mid- to late summer and early fall. (These storms can occur any month of the year [but more often in summer] in the western North Pacific, and there are none in the South Atlantic and few in the eastern South Pacific.) The illustration shows in a very general way typical hurricane tracks affecting the

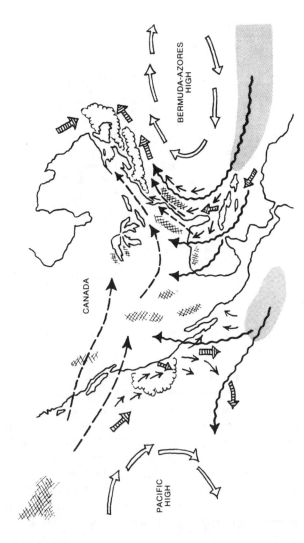

Fig. 8-3. Generalized U.S. weather during the boating season. See key on facing page.

BERMUDA-AZORES
HIGH

CANADA

PACIFIC
HIGH

Key

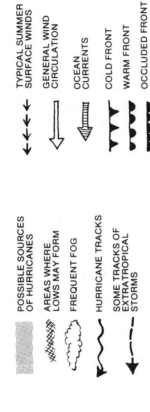

POSSIBLE SOURCES OF HURRICANES	
AREAS WHERE LOWS MAY FORM	
FREQUENT FOG	
HURRICANE TRACKS	
SOME TRACKS OF EXTRATROPICAL STORMS	

TYPICAL SUMMER SURFACE WINDS	
GENERAL WIND CIRCULATION	
OCEAN CURRENTS	
COLD FRONT	
WARM FRONT	
OCCLUDED FRONT	

United States and areas where tropical lows are most apt to originate. Notice that hurricanes are usually born in hot, humid regions, and they move westward in the trade wind belt but then drift northward until reaching the prevailing westerlies where they curve (meteorologists say "recurve") to the east. It should be kept firmly in mind that the illustrated tracks are highly idealized, and actual tracks are often very erratic, especially when influenced by changeable low and high pressure atmospheric conditions.

— Anticyclonic gales, i.e., strong winds from highs, are rare, but they can occur when a high is asymmetrical, with the center aloft not directly over the center at ground level. This produces tightly packed isobars (lines of equal pressure) on one side and indicates strong winds. In addition, there are thunderstorm highs caused by the falling of cold air, which increases the pressure. Then too, the filling in of pressure after passage of a cold front can produce very strong winds. Heed the old proverb: "First rise after low portends a stronger blow."

STORM AVOIDANCE

— Well before getting underway, check the overall weather pattern on television, radio, newspaper, etc., and observe the movement of your barometer if you have one at home. Everyone knows that weather reports cannot be relied on absolutely, because there are so many variables in atmospheric conditions that can block, speed up, or alter the predicted movement of weather systems. However, a synoptic forecast and knowledge of the general weather (the location of highs, lows, and fronts) to the west of you (in middle latitudes) combined with local observations of the barometer, wind, and sky can tell you with reasonable accuracy what to expect in your locality.

— Radio weather forecasts from the National Weather Service (NWS) are broadcast continuously and updated every few hours on VHF-FM on frequencies ranging from 162.4 to 162.55 MHz. These are invaluable for coastal sailors. Offshore sailors can obtain hourly high seas reports on WWV (2.5, 5, 10, 15, and 20 MHz) or WWVH (2.5, 5, and 10 MHz). Also pay attention to storm warning signals in the form of flags or lights displayed at yacht clubs, weather stations, or elsewhere (see illustration).

— A barometer, which measures atmospheric pressure, should be on every cruising boat. Little can be told by one glance at a barometer. It must be read over a period of time, noting the position of the inside needle on an aneroid barometer about every hour in order to record the pressure trend. A steadily falling glass (barometer) indicates unsettled rainy weather especially when the wind is from easterly quadrants. A rapid fall indicates an approaching low and stormy weather. A rapid rise, especially with falling temperature, usually means high winds. An old tradition is to tap the glass to read its trend, but this only works if the needle is slightly stuck.

— Air-mass thunderstorms are best avoided in coastal waters by keeping an eye out for rising cumulus clouds with firm edges in the western sky (in middle latitudes) on a hot, humid afternoon. Also listen for static on an AM radio. When you see a westerly thunderhead developing, the safest policy is to head for a harbor or protected windward shore where you can anchor. Otherwise, obtain plenty of sea room (distance from a lee shore), and be prepared to lower sail at a moment's notice.

— Lightning is a concern during thunderstorms. See that your boat is properly grounded (refer to Chapter 1). Small boats without masts can be protected by a jury mast such as a telescoping metal boathook electrically connected to

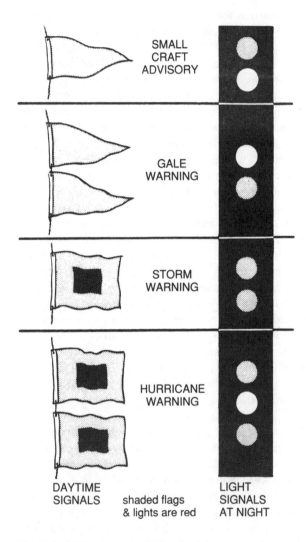

SMALL CRAFT ADVISORY

GALE WARNING

STORM WARNING

HURRICANE WARNING

DAYTIME SIGNALS

shaded flags & lights are red

LIGHT SIGNALS AT NIGHT

Fig. 8-4. Storm warning signals

an outboard motor. This will provide an umbrella-like cone of protection for crew sitting aft fairly near (but not close to) the motor. On cabin cruisers during electrical storms, the crew should go below when possible. They should not hold onto rigging or metal objects. If there is a metal wheel, try to anchor to avoid the need for a helmsman, or use the autopilot if there is one. Otherwise, the helmsman can be protected with rubber gloves or a gripping device such as a piece of foam rubber.

— The approach of a warm front usually gives ample advanced warning with a lot of cirrus (whispy, high-altitude clouds) a day or more before the front's arrival, then cirrostratus (a whitish sheet that causes a large ring around the sun or moon), then perhaps altostratus (a thicker gray sheet at middle altitudes), and finally nimbostratus (low, dark, rain clouds) or cumulonimbus in unstable air. After passage of the warm front, one should be prepared for the possibly imminent arrival of the following cold front, often with thunderstorms preceding it.

— Crosswind rules (written about by meterologist Alan Watts) can provide valuable clues about your position with regard to a nearby extratropical low. These rules involve observation of the winds aloft (as shown by the movement of high-altitude clouds) and comparing them with surface winds. Stand with your back to the surface wind, and if the upper clouds approach from your left, you are probably in the path of the low (in the Northern Hemisphere). Upper clouds approaching from your right (while standing back-to-wind) indicate clearing weather. Upper and lower winds moving in the same direction with warm temperature indicates you are south of the low and might expect a cold front. Opposing upper and lower winds show that you are directly north of the low, and you can expect improving weather.

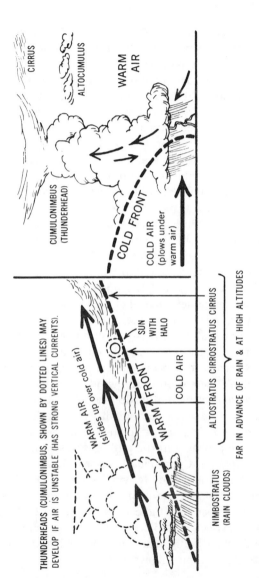

Fig. 8-5. Fronts and associated clouds

CIRRUS

ALTOCUMULUS

WARM AIR

CUMULONIMBUS
(THUNDERHEAD)

COLD FRONT

COLD AIR
(plows under warm air)

THUNDERHEADS (CUMULONIMBUS, SHOWN BY DOTTED LINES) MAY
DEVELOP IF AIR IS UNSTABLE (HAS STRONG VERTICAL CURRENTS).

SUN WITH
HALO

WARM AIR
(slides up over cold air)

WARM FRONT

COLD AIR

ALTOSTRATUS CIRROSTRATUS CIRRUS

FAR IN ADVANCE OF RAIN & AT HIGH ALTITUDES

NIMBOSTRATUS
(RAIN CLOUDS)

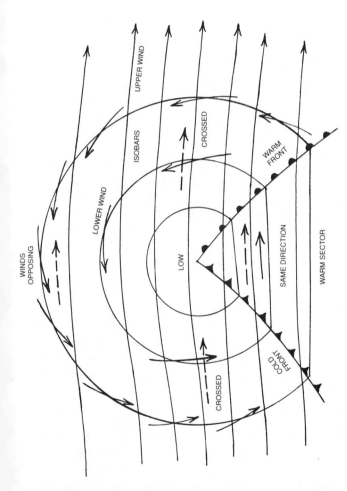

Fig. 8-6. Cross wind rules (based on diagram by Alan Watts)

—Buys Ballot's law is commonly used to locate a low: stand facing the surface wind, and the low pressure center will be about 112 degrees to your right (in the northern hemisphere). A rough measurement of 112 degrees can be obtained by extending your right arm so that it is horizontal and then moving it back as far as you comfortably can while keeping your shoulders square to the wind.

—Hurricanes are best avoided by being alert to hurricane reports during the season, especially from August to mid-October in the United States. In fact, it is prudent to stay reasonably close to protected harbors during the peak of the hurricane season.

—At sea or along a coast the first sign of a hurricane is often the arrival of long swells (with a period between crests of perhaps fifteen or more seconds) coming from the general direction of the storm. These can be seen or felt in fair weather with relatively cloudless skies a day or two or more before the storm's arrival. A clockwise change in the direction of the swell in the Northern Hemisphere indicates the storm center is passing from left to right—from right to left with a counterclockwise change in swell direction.

—The next warning sign of a hurricane may be the arrival of mare's tails (high-altitude cirrus) followed by a sequence of clouds not unlike that of a warm front. Sometimes there are precursor bands of thunderstorms quite far ahead of the storm.

—The most dangerous part of a hurricane is its right front quadrant (facing the direction in which the storm is moving), partly because that is where the winds are increased by the storm's movement, the largest swells are generated there, and a vessel in that area is most apt to be blown into the storm's eye (where seas are chaotic). Should you have the misfortune of being caught directly

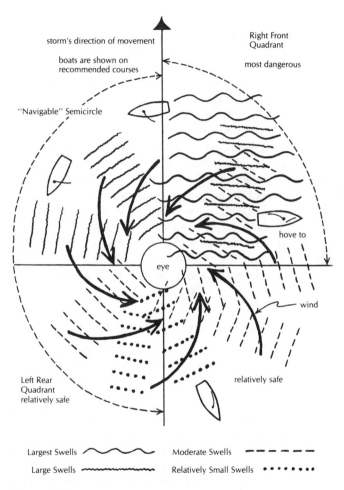

storm's direction of movement

boats are shown on recommended courses

"Navigable" Semicircle

Right Front Quadrant

most dangerous

hove to

eye

wind

Left Rear Quadrant relatively safe

relatively safe

Largest Swells	Moderate Swells
Large Swells	Relatively Small Swells

Fig. 8-7. Hurricane strategy for Northern Hemisphere (From Sea Sense *by Richard Henderson)*

in the path of a hurricane, head for the navigable semicircle (the left half of the storm) where conditions are more moderate. Generalized recommended courses for boats caught in the vicinity of a hurricane are illustrated. Management of the boat would actually depend to a large extent on how the boat is positioned with respect to the seas, and this will be discussed in the following section.

—Your location with respect to a hurricane can be estimated with reasonable accuracy by using Buys Ballot's law (previously described) along with the barometer. A veering wind (shifting clockwise) in the Northern Hemisphere shows you are in the right-hand semicircle, while a backing wind (shifting counterclockwise) shows you are in the left-hand semicircle. When the wind direction is steady but with increasing velocity and the barometer is falling, the storm is headed toward you. Steady wind direction with diminishing velocity and rising glass indicates the storm is moving away.

STORMY WEATHER BOAT HANDLING AND TACTICS

How a vessel is handled in heavy weather will depend to a large extent on such factors as the kind of blow encountered, the size and design of the vessel, and sea conditions.

—In heavy weather where the boat is laboring but can continue sailing or proceeding towards her destination under power, the usual recommendation is to slow down. About the only exception to this rule is when running off before following seas that are not overly confused and when steering is difficult at slow speed.

—In the above conditions a high-speed powerboat with small rudder(s) and a very unbalanced hull (fine forward and full aft) often can be controlled more easily by riding on the back of a fairly regular wave at a speed that will maintain her position. As noted in Chapter 4, powerboats should always be turned to avoid taking steep, breaking seas on the beam.

—Unless they are racing perhaps, sailboats in moderately heavy weather should have their sail reduced not only to slow down and minimize risk of damage from pounding and being swept by seas, but also to reduce heeling and possibly broaching to (inadvertently rounding up into the wind). Nowadays sail reduction is usually accomplished with jiffy reefing for boomed sails and roller furling for jibs (see Chapter 2 under "Sail Tips").

—Jiffy reefing is often rigged as illustrated, with a hook at the tack and a clew earing (reef line) secured to the boom directly under the cringle (grommet), then led up to the cringle, down to the cheek block at the boom's end, and forward to a winch. To reef, the sheet is slacked, sail is lowered until the reef cringle or ring on the luff can be attached on the tack hook, the luff is tightened with the halyard, then the leech cringle is hauled down to the boom and winched taut. Although seldom vital, the bunt (loose part of the sail hanging down) can be lashed to the boom with reef points (short lines rove through eyelets in the sail) or a long lacing line. When possible, pass the reef points between the sail's foot and the boom; otherwise, use a spirally wrapped lacing line to distribute strain at the foot more evenly. Obviously, a topping lift (or its equivalent) is needed to hold up the boom while reefing.

—If a cruiser is fitted with a roller furling/reefing jib, it is a wise practice to have an inner forestay (preferably detachable for easy tacking in fair weather) that will accept a hanked-on storm staysail. The staysail will be easier to handle than a jib and keep the boat in balance (see Chapter 2).

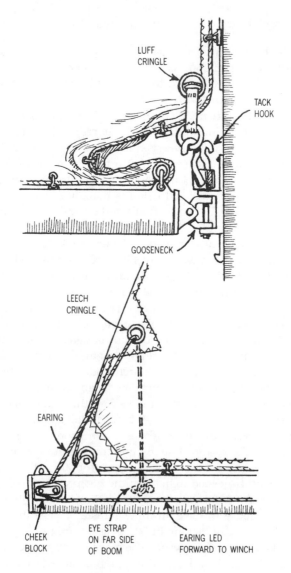

Fig. 8-8. Jiffy reefing (details at tack and clew)

Fig. 8-9. Inner forestay for Spitfire staysail

—An important requirement for sudden squalls such as thunderstorms and microbursts is the ability to achieve watertight integrity and lower sail quickly. Whenever a squall is threatening or conditions seem ripe for a sudden blow, close all ports and any hatches that are not on the boat's centerline. When there is a low companionway sill, insert and lock in the lower drop board (slide). Reduce sail early and be ready to lower sails at a moment's notice. Keep lines coiled so they are ready to run, and see that sheets are cleated inboard so that they will not be underwater during a knockdown.

—Very often the right tactic for a violent short-lived storm is to lower all sail and power slowly into the seas until the blow subsides. If the boat has no power or it is insufficient to hold the bow up and there is ample searoom to leeward, you can run off under bare poles. When there is a nearby windward shore it often makes sense to anchor, especially before electrical storms, but rarely should you anchor on a lee shore unless you're unable to "claw off" (move away from the shore).

—A prolonged storm such as one produced by a slow moving low pressure system should give plenty of warning and allow a coastal boat to reach port. Onboard an offshore boat, preparations should be made well in advance of the foul weather. Bear in mind that tasks performed while the weather is still fair are infinitely easier than during the storm. Take seasickness remedies well in advance, don foul weather gear, rig jack lines for safety harnesses, secure all loose gear, break out storm sails, don flotation jackets, prepare food and drinks that might be needed, and locate all gear that could be useful.

—During a prolonged blow offshore when the weather deteriorates to the extent that a boat under reduced sail is

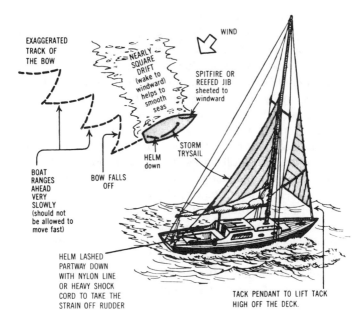

Fig. 8-10. Heaving to

at risk to damage, a well accepted tactic is heaving-to. The standard method of doing so is illustrated. Notice that the sails are trimmed to oppose each other (with jib or staysail aback) thereby stopping significant headway. The helm is lashed down (rudder to windward) so that when the boat gains headway she luffs up until the backed headsail becomes the predominant force causing the bow to fall off as shown in the illustration. It is best to have a loose-footed storm trysail similar to the one illustrated, but a deeply reefed mainsail will do. The boat's drift wake to windward tends to make steep seas break before they strike the hull.

—If the boat or sails are being excessively punished by heaving to, she might successfully run off under bare poles or with a storm jib trimmed flat. Opinions vary as to optimal speed when scudding (running off). Some racing boats have had success running at high speeds, but they are normally light displacement craft that create small hull waves, manned by a number of highly skilled helmsmen who might effectively steer to avoid dangerous following seas for hour after hour. Heavy displacement craft that make large hull waves, which could reinforce the following seas, are usually safer at slower speeds, especially when there is a shortage of skilled helmsmen. Nevertheless, there should be sufficient speed for good rudder control—perhaps a speed equal to the square root of the boat's waterline length, depending on her individual design. Speed can be controlled by towing drags astern (lines, sails, anchors, tires, etc.). A popular modern drogue (drag) is the Galerider (see illustration), which is similar to

Fig. 8-11. Galerider drogue

the loosely woven basket drogues used by the ancient Chinese. A milk crate or two also make an effective drag.

— A more controversial tactic is lying ahull, whereby the boat is stripped of all sail and, with helm normally lashed alee (rudder to windward), is allowed to drift freely and find her own position. Most boats will lie about beam-to the seas. Advantages of this tactic are that the boat maximizes her buoyancy, yields to the smash of seas, and minimizes headway. Lying ahull can be done with minimal effort and allows the crew to retire belowdecks. Disadvantages are that the boat may roll a lot, and there is the possibility of a rollover (capsize) or a heavy sea smashing the cabin top. In the worst weather all hatches, ports, and vents should be closed, and the crew should be lashed or belted in their bunks.

— Lying ahull can be a very effective and comfortable tactic in the right conditions, but I would not try it unless the boat had a high range of stability, at least over 130 degrees (see Chapter 1), and had a well crowned (curved) cabin top that was well supported. Nor would I lie ahull in plunging seas (steep waves that topple as opposed to longer waves with whitecaps). Powerboats without ballast should seldom if ever lie ahull in breaking seas. A better tactic is to power slowly into the seas or run off before them.

— Plunging seas usually are produced by shallow water, especially a rapidly shoaling bottom which can produce overfalls (turbulent breakers that are particularly dangerous for small craft). Ocean waves can "feel bottom" and become steep even fairly far offshore above a continental shelf. In deep water, waves tend to produce less dangerous spilling breakers (waves that break at the top of their crests) unless they are in the area of a strong offshore current, such as the Gulf Stream. The steepest seas are usually produced when the current opposes the wind. If possible, an offshore boat expecting heavy weather should head toward deep water and away from a strong current. Confused seas often can be expected after a drastic wind shift.

— An offshore boat that has a relatively low range of stability such as a powerboat, multihull, or beamy centerboarder with a high center of gravity, should be equipped with a sea anchor or sizable drogue to help hold the boat end-to the seas when progress can't be made in extremely heavy weather. The most familiar sea anchors take the form of a parachute or large cone. Many modern boats with underbodies cutaway forward will not readily lie to a sea anchor streamed from the bow, although a riding sail (a small, flat sail set on the backstay, or mizzen) may help. When the boat will not lie to a sea anchor from the bow, a drogue might be streamed from the stern but only if the boat has a small cockpit with sizable drains, ample freeboard, and complete watertight integrity aft.

— Perhaps the most effective drogue to date for survival conditions in an extreme offshore storm is the series drogue (a series of small cones evenly spaced along the anchor line). After extensive testing by its inventor, Donald Jordan, and the U.S. Coast Guard, the series drogue (called Sea Grabber by one producer) has shown that it will keep more or less continuous tension on the anchor line, thus holding the boat's end almost constantly toward the seas with minimal jerking and yawing. A conventional anchor, weighing about 25 pounds, is secured to the end of the line, and it is recommended that the drogue be streamed from a bridle at the stern (see illustration). Should the boat turn broadside to a breaking wave, the bridle will exert a powerful pull which will turn the stern toward the sea.

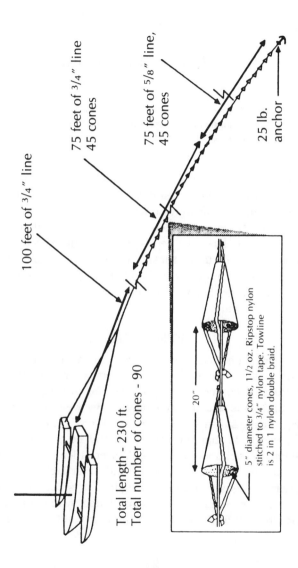

100 feet of ³/₄" line

75 feet of ³/₄" line
45 cones

75 feet of ⁵/₈" line,
45 cones

25 lb.
anchor

Total length - 230 ft.
Total number of cones - 90

20"

5" diameter cones, 1½ oz. Ripstop nylon stitched to ³/₄" nylon tape. Towline is 2 in 1 nylon double braid.

Fig. 8-12. Series drogue (Courtesy Donald Jordan and U.S. Coast Guard)

9. Anchoring and Mooring

And I advise all sound cruisers to anchor properly in a harbor, not tie up at a 'marina,' the yachtsmen's slum. —Samuel Eliot Morison

There are several advantages to anchoring rather than tying up, the main one being greater privacy, but the key word in Admiral Morison's advice is "properly." Improper anchoring has caused difficult and quite often embarrassing situations. Even the best sailors may have occasional problems, but certainly these can be minimized by carrying the right ground tackle (anchoring gear), choosing a good anchorage, following accepted procedures, and anchoring with care.

GROUND TACKLE

Every cruising boat should carry at least three anchors: a lunch hook (small anchor for temporary use in fair weather); a worker (working anchor for overnight use in all conditions except extremely heavy weather); and a large, heavy storm anchor. An old rule of thumb for anchor weight is that the worker should be one pound of weight for each foot of the boat's overall length, but this depends on the type of anchor and other factors. Some modern designs can be much lighter. It is best to follow the weight recommendations published by anchor manufacturers. If in doubt, err on the heavy side. It is often recommended that the lunch hook be a size smaller than the worker and the storm anchor a size larger, but the latter should be the largest size that conveniently can be handled. The following anchor types are the ones most often used by the U.S. boater today:

—The *yachtsman* (or fisherman) anchor is a traditional type with hook-like arms and a sliding stock which locks in place with a key (see illustration for terminology of parts). This is a good general-purpose anchor, but it should weigh more for equivalent holding power than more modern types (soon to be described). It is perhaps least effective in soft mud because of the small area of its fluke. The most obvious fault of the yachtsman is that when one fluke is buried, the other one sticks up and might be fouled by the rode (anchor line) during a wind shift or change of current. A boat anchored with a yachtsman should not be left unwatched over a period of time, because several 180 degree wind or current shifts could completely wrap the exposed fluke and break out the anchor. The yachtsman type least subject to this problem is the Herreshoff anchor, which has more diamond-shaped flukes. Be sure the bills are reasonably sharp for effective burying in hard bottoms. The yachtsman is usually effective in weed covered bottoms and is probably the most likely anchor to become hooked in rocky seabeds. There is at least one type of yachtsman (by Paul Luke) that can be disassembled for easy stowage. This feature makes it ideal for a heavy storm anchor that can easily be stowed in the bilge and assembled on deck when it is needed.

—The *plow*, an English design shaped like a farmer's plow, is considered by many experienced sailors to be the most versatile anchor because it is effective in a great variety of seabeds. However, it is seldom as satisfactory as

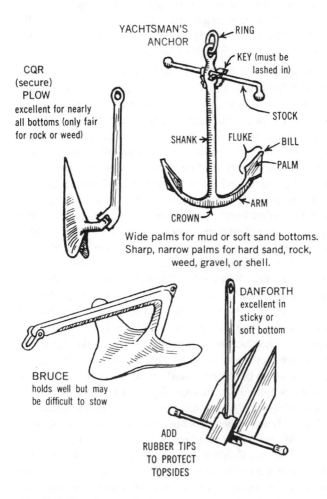

YACHTSMAN'S ANCHOR

RING

KEY (must be lashed in)

STOCK

SHANK

FLUKE

BILL

PALM

ARM

CROWN

CQR (secure) PLOW
excellent for nearly all bottoms (only fair for rock or weed)

Wide palms for mud or soft sand bottoms. Sharp, narrow palms for hard sand, rock, weed, gravel, or shell.

DANFORTH
excellent in sticky or soft bottom

BRUCE
holds well but may be difficult to stow

ADD RUBBER TIPS TO PROTECT TOPSIDES

Fig. 9-1. Popular anchors

the yachtsman anchor in heavy weed or rocky bottoms. Despite being a burying anchor, the plow can drag in very soft ooze, as I have discovered from firsthand experience. The original English design called CQR ("secure") has been imitated successfully by a few companies such as Danforth but unsuccessfully by some others. A unique feature of the plow is that the shank is swiveled where it joins the flukes, and this allows the anchor to remain buried during a moderate wind shift. According to impartial tests (in sandy bottoms) the plow is relatively effective when it is necessary to anchor at short scope (scope is the length of rode being used). Plows are difficult to stow on deck, but they can be kept in lockers or preferably stowed on projecting bow rollers where they are readily available for easy handling.

—The *Danforth* (fluke type), used so effectively by landing craft in World War II, is a relatively lightweight anchor with large flukes that are hinged at the shank. It is an excellent anchor for sand or mud bottoms, but its flukes can become jammed with weeds, shells, or garbage lying on the bottom. The most effective Danforth in most conditions is the Hi-Tensile Deepset, which has a semiflexible shank and thin, sharp flukes, but it may bury so deeply that recovery can be difficult. An extra light Danforth type is the aluminum *Fortress*, which holds extremely well once it digs in, but is best used with a length of heavy chain to add weight. The fluke/shank angle of the Fortress can be changed for optimal use in sand or mud. It is not recommended for hard clay or grass. A Danforth can be stowed quite easily on deck, on a pulpit, or on a bow roller. A minor disadvantage is that the Danforth will not always sink directly to the bottom but may tend to plane when the vessel is moving.

—The *Bruce* is a solid (unhinged, nonswiveling) stockless anchor with spoonlike flukes that has been used effectively on offshore oil rigs. It is perhaps the strongest anchor and holds well in most bottoms once dug in. Like the plow it holds relatively well on short scope and does not readily break out when the wind shifts. An obvious drawback of the Bruce is difficult stowage; however, it can be operated quite easily from a bow roller.

There are many other types of anchors, but the ones just discussed are the most popular and widely accepted. Some folding anchors such as the *Northhill* and the folding *grapnel* have proven convenient for less than stormy weather use. The *Flook* is a specialty anchor that will glide through the water when thrown overboard. It is good for a stern anchor or for kedging off after a grounding. The *Delta* is a solid (nonswiveling) plow that works well from a bow roller and is said to be effective in weedy as well as other bottoms, although it may not stay put as well as the *CQR* type during a wind or current shift.

The most commonly used anchor rodes (cables) are nylon line or chain. The latter has an advantage in resistance to chafe and, because of its weight, chain provides a catenary (sag in the rode) which increases the anchor's holding power. Most small craft yachtsmen, however, prefer nylon, because it is easier to handle and provides elasticity to reduce shock loading which can break out an anchor. If there is a problem with chafe, it can be alleviated by using a chafe guard of rubber or neoprene hose at the bow chock and a leader (short length) of chain between the anchor and rode. In some areas with coral or sharp rocks on the bottom a long chain leader may be needed. The end of an anchor line should have an eye splice around a metal thimble to prevent chafe from the shackle. When it is necessary to tie an anchor to a shackle or ring use a fisherman's bend (see illustration) or bowline with an extra turn around the shackle or ring. Small- to medium-size cruisers should carry at least 200 feet of rode for the working anchor.

Be sure the attachment point for the rode on your boat is secure. Bow cleats should be large enough for adquately wrapping and hitching a large diameter line, and of course, cleats should be through bolted to below deck structural members and have large backing plates. A bitt or Samson post (vertical mooring/anchor post)

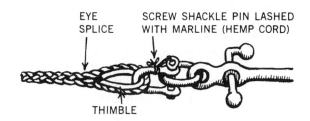

EYE SPLICE

SCREW SHACKLE PIN LASHED WITH MARLINE (HEMP CORD)

THIMBLE

Fig. 9-2. Anchor line thimble and shackle

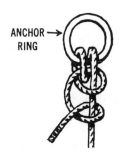

ANCHOR → RING

Fig. 9-3. Fisherman's bend

should extend to the stem or keel so that the load is distributed to the hull rather than only the deck. Anchor windlasses should be equally well supported. Chocks (through which the rode is led) should be positioned so that the rode is fairled (led as straight as possible), and they should be round and smooth to minimize chafe.

ANCHORING TECHNIQUE

Select an anchorage with care. Study your charts to see if there is sufficient depth of water and the anchorage affords good protection. Take into consideration the state of the tide, which can be determined from tide tables or quite often by studying watermarks on fixed channel markers, piers, and the shoreline. When estimating the amount of protection a harbor affords, consider not only the present wind direction, but also the likelihood of a shift. Listen to weather reports and observe the sky (see Chapter 8). Another consideration is the surge from swells entering the harbor. Waves will tend to bend around a point, and you might lie to the wind but take the swells on your beam, which may cause an uncomfortable roll.

—After entering a harbor, move around it to determine where the best spot is to anchor. Considerations are: proximity to any spot where you might want to go ashore, protection during the possible arrival of bad weather, good holding ground, ample depth of water, distance from other anchored boats to assure sufficient swinging room in the event of a wind shift, and distance away from channels and boat traffic.

—When you have decided where to anchor, it is usually best to head into the wind, put the engine in reverse (if it is running) to stop forward motion, and lower (don't throw) the anchor from the bow. Keep tension on the rode until after the boat starts moving backwards to prevent the rode from fouling the anchor. Then slowly pay out scope and give an occasional momentary pull on the line until you can feel the flukes dig in. If the bow begins to fall off (move away from the wind), keep tension on the rode until the boat comes nearly head-to-wind. Then back down to bury the anchor. In a crowded anchorage you might be able to shorten scope slightly after you are assured the anchor is buried.

—If anchoring to windward of another boat, be sure to go far enough upwind to allow paying out plenty of rode to cope with the possible arrival of bad weather.

—Scope is the name of the game when it comes to security at anchor. In former times the scope-to-depth ratio usually recommended was 7 to 1, but in today's crowded harbors a 5 to 1 ratio is often the best you can hope for. To achieve a decent ratio, anchor in the shallowest water you can without fear of grounding at low tide. This will also get you away from large boats of deep draft.

—Hand signals should be given to the helmsman by the person handling the anchor on the bow. Normally the anchor person points to the left or right to indicate which way to steer. A hand held straight up indicates that the gear should be in neutral, while a wave in the forward direction (palm of hand facing forward) means come ahead, and a wave in the backwards direction (palm facing aft) means to back up (engine in reverse).

—To break out a buried anchor, haul in the rode until it is at short stay (straight up and down). Then snub the rode (temporarily secure it with a turn around the cleat or bitt) and allow the boat's motion to lift up the shank and apply leverage to the buried fluke(s). Sometimes the boat's forward momentum, resulting from taking in the rode, will supply enough force, but in stubborn cases the engine (or sails) must be used to drive the boat ahead. Some deep burying anchors such as the Danforth Deepset might be broken out by a combination of driving the boat ahead and then backwards while at short stay. On small boats in very stubborn cases, it might be helpful to move all crew forward, take in all possible scope, and then move the crew aft when driving ahead.

—When anchoring in rocky bottoms or where there are abandoned mooring chains or cables that could seriously snag the anchor, it is often advisable to rig a trip line and buoy. The trip line is tied to the anchor's crown and supported by a buoy almost directly above the anchor. When a fouled anchor cannot be freed by hauling up the rode, it usually can be broken out by pulling up on the trip line. The problem with this system is that the buoy is occasionally picked up by another boat or the line may be cut by the propeller of a passing boat. To avoid this problem, you can eliminate the buoy and tie the end of the trip line to the rode where it can be reached when the rode is hauled up at short stay.

—If an anchor is fouled but no trip line is rigged the crown can sometimes be snagged with a piece of chain dropped down the vertical rode (when it is at short stay). Danforth or Flook anchors might be cleared when hooked under a piece of cable or chain by winching up the anchor until it is well clear of the bottom and then quickly slacking the rode and allowing the anchor to glide free (see illustration). A fouled plow often can be cleared by powering directly to windward of it.

—In stormy weather or other difficult conditions, it may be necessary to deploy more than one anchor. Sometimes a second anchor is used in tandem with the first on a single rode. The second anchor might be shackled to the

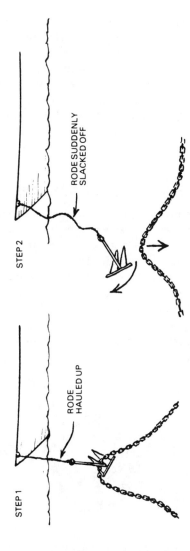

STEP 1

RODE HAULED UP

STEP 2

RODE SUDDENLY SLACKED OFF

Fig. 9-4 Clearing a fouled Danforth or flook

end of the chain leader and be used either to increase the number of buried or partially buried flukes or to add weight to the rode for a more effective catenary. Another technique that helps prevent extreme yawing is the hammerlock system, utilizing a second anchor at shorter scope out of tandem with the primary anchor at an angle of from 45 to 90 degrees. A flat cut riding sail hoisted aft (perhaps on the permanent backstay) and sheeted flat will also help prevent yawing at anchor (see illustration).

MISCELLANEOUS ANCHOR TIPS

— For maximum elasticity of anchor line (to relieve shock loading) don't use excessively heavy line. Nylon line of moderate diameter is a good choice, and three strand twisted construction provides the most stretch.

— Chain rode is very good until it is stretched taut, and then its lack of give will cause severe shock loading. To alleviate this problem, use a chain hook secured to a long piece of light nylon line that holds slack in the chain. Hook on forward of the bow and lead the line through a

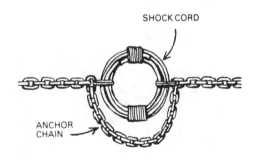

Fig. 9-5. Relieving shock loading on chain with shock cord

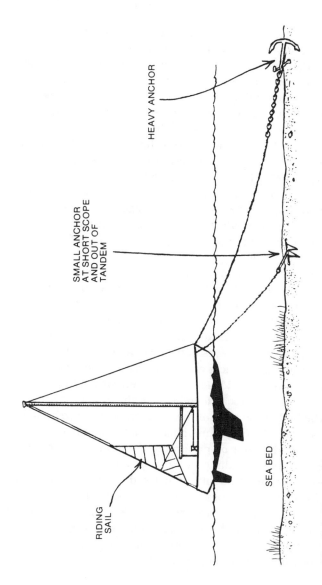

RIDING SAIL

SMALL ANCHOR
AT SHORT SCOPE
AND OUT OF
TANDEM

HEAVY ANCHOR

SEA BED

Fig. 9-6. Yaw control at anchor

bow chock and all the way aft to a large sheet winch. Then crank in the line to put slack in the chain. Another partial solution is to use a rubber snubber (obtainable at chandleries) or use a coil of shock cord as illustrated. When there is no windlass to service a chain rode, it is especially important to have a pawl at the bow roller to hold the chain when it is being hauled in.

—If your boat has a bowsprit, beware of chafe from the anchor rode on the bobstay. Usually the anchor roller should be at the end of the bowsprit. Be sure that the bodies of projecting bow rollers extend far enough inboard for adequate fastenings and leverage to provide security when the boat is violently pitching and yawing. There should be a retaining pin to prevent the rode from jumping off the roller.

—If your boat is subject to hobbyhorsing (extreme pitching in a head sea), try to reduce anchor weight on the bow. A heavy storm anchor normally carried on the foredeck should be lashed on the cabin top or preferably in the bilge as close as possible amidships, and chain should not be stowed in the very eyes of the boat (all the way forward).

—Be sure all anchors carried on deck, in bow rollers, and even those carried below are securely lashed in place.

—The bitter (inboard) end of a chain should be securely attached to the base of the Samson post or eye bolted to a sturdy structural member, but the chain should be lashed with line or preferably a coil of shock cord (to relieve shock loading) that can be cut in an emergency.

—Anchor rodes should be marked, normally with paint on a chain or thongs on a line, to show the amount of scope that is out. Important marks begin at a scope equivalent to the boat's draft through a scope equal to about seven times the depth of water with the marks occuring about every fathom (six feet).

—Screw pins for anchor shackles should be tightened with a marlinespike or the equivalent, and be lashed to prevent unscrewing.

— Use rubber cane tips on the end of Danforth stocks (and wherever else you can) to prevent anchors from scarring the topsides, rails, or decks when bringing them aboard.

—When entering a harbor to anchor, study the directions in which the rodes of other boats lead. One boat might be lying to the wind while another might be affected by the current. The position of boats and lead of their rodes will give you a clue as to which way the boats will swing and where the strongest current is running.

— Use your depth-sounder or lead-line to determine the depth of water before anchoring. A lead-line can be armed (have its bottom cavity filled with tallow, soap, or grease) to pick up samples of the seabed so that you can determine its physical characteristics. Remember that bottom characteristics in some areas are marked on the chart with certain abbreviations such as M (for mud), rky (for rocky), S (for sand), sft. (for soft), Grs. (for grass), hrd. (for hard), Sh. (for shells), stk. (for sticky), etc.

— If your boat has a cutaway forefoot and a lot of windage forward so that the bow is quickly blown off before you can back down to set the anchor, try casting anchor while moving ahead downwind. This can effectively cause the anchor to dig in, but beware of scarring the topsides if you have a chain rode.

— If mosquitoes or other insects are a problem, try anchoring further offshore, especially in a location where there is more breeze.

— After anchoring and adjusting scope, always take bearings on fixed objects on shore or channel markers to establish ranges or fix your position. Later you can check the bearings or ranges to see that you are not dragging.

—If dragging cannot be stopped by letting out all possible scope, you might try a kellet. This consists of a weight such as a pig of lead (with an eyebolt) held on a rope rode with a large shackle or carbine (locking) snaphook that allows the kellet to slide slightly more than halfway down the rode to increase the catenary. The kellet is held in place and retrieved with a light, preferably buoyant, re-trieving line leading from the kellet to the bow. When ex-pecting a very heavy blow, it might be wise to shackle the kellet to the end of a long chain leader where it joins the nylon rode.

—When it is found, after a wind shift, for example, that two anchored boats are too close for comfort, it is up to the last arrival to move unless the first arrival is dragging her anchor.

—When there is concern about chafe of the anchor line on an abrasive bottom despite a long chain leader, you can use a buoy to lift the line off the bottom.

—Chafe at the bow chock can be alleviated with chafing gear such as neoprene hoses or by frequently altering the scope so that the rubbing occurs at different spots on the anchor line.

—A yachtsman anchor fouled in a rocky bottom might be cleared by circling the anchor, thus wrapping the exposed fluke with the rode, and then lifting the anchor by its fluke.

—When weighing anchor, mud is most effectively re-moved by vigorously dunking the anchor. This can be ac-complished when the anchor is not too heavy, by leaning over the bow with one elbow on a knee (to alleviate stress on the back), while the other arm dunks the anchor in and out of the water. Allow the muddy end of the rode to drag overboard. Have a swab and draw the bucket up forward. Large boats may need a washdown hose to clean the ground tackle as it comes aboard.

—Whether or not you use two anchors (see "Anchoring Technique") a flat-cut riding sail set all the way aft will be most helpful in preventing the boat from ranging around her anchor and yawing.

—If your working anchor is over 35 pounds, you'll probably want a windlass. When it is electrically or hydraulically powered, be sure there is a practical manual backup system of operation, such as a long cranking handle that allows good leverage and, when the drum axis is horizontal, make sure you have the ability to stand up when cranking.

—To kedge off after running aground (see Chapter 7), carry your anchor out in a dinghy with the rode coiled in the sternsheets (aftermost part of an open boat) and its end made fast to the vessel so that the rode runs out as the boat is rowed away. When there is no dinghy, the kedge anchor might be floated on life preservers, or a light kedge such as a Fortress might be thrown, or a gliding anchor such as the Flook might be used.

MOORING

The term mooring (securing a vessel) can be applied either to berthing or anchoring. In the latter sense it means a semipermanent anchoring system or one where there are multiple anchors with rodes leading in opposite directions (or nearly so).

Permanent Moorings

There are a number of systems for so-called permanent moorings. Some use multiple anchors and a few use bow and stern anchors (when swinging room is restricted), but the system illustrated is the norm for reasonable holding bottom, average tide, and sufficient swinging room. A per-

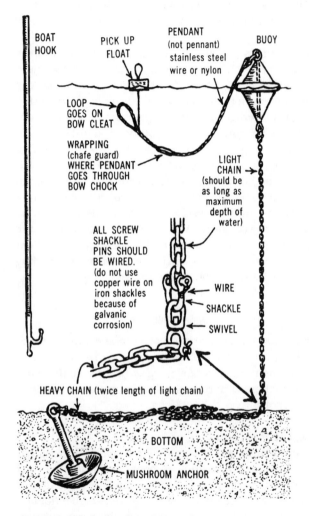

BOAT
HOOK

PICK UP
FLOAT

PENDANT
(not pennant)
stainless steel
wire or nylon

BUOY

LOOP
GOES ON
BOW CLEAT

WRAPPING
(chafe guard)
WHERE PENDANT
GOES THROUGH
BOW CHOCK

LIGHT
CHAIN →
(should be
as long as
maximum
depth of
water)

ALL SCREW
SHACKLE
PINS SHOULD
BE WIRED.
(do not use
copper wire on
iron shackles
because of
galvanic
corrosion)

WIRE

SHACKLE

SWIVEL

HEAVY CHAIN (twice length of light chain)

BOTTOM

MUSHROOM ANCHOR

Fig. 9-7. Permanent mooring

manent (or semipermanent) anchor such as the mushroom type illustrated should weigh almost 100 pounds for every 10 feet of boat length.

The rode has a long heavy chain connected to a lighter chain with a heavy swivel to avoid twisting. Note that screw shackle pins should be wired, and the wire and cotter pins should be of metals compatible with the shackles to avoid galvanic corrosion. The light chain is about equal to the maximum depth of water, while heavy chain, which lies on the bottom, should be at least one and a half times longer but preferably twice as long.

The mooring buoy has a solid rod connecting the upper and lower eyes. Attached to the upper eye is a pendant, usually of nylon, which has a large loop spliced into its far end to fit over the bow cleat. The pendant should be about 2½ times the boat's freeboard at the bow. A pickup float is attached to the loop with light line. The float illustrated requires a boathook for pickup, but many floats have plastic staffs sticking up to obviate the need for a boathook and afford better visibility for the helmsman. One advantage in having a boathook is that it provides a longer reach should the boat's bow blow off after headway has been stopped. As mentioned in Chapter 6, a mooring buoy is white with a blue horizontal band.

Bahamian Moor

When swinging room is limited and there is a strong tidal current that reverses direction with flood and ebb tide, it may be desirable to use a Bahamian moor, whereby two anchors are set out in opposite directions in line with the current flow (see illustration). An easy way to moor in this manner is to drop the first anchor while going ahead and pay out all or most of your scope; then drop the second anchor, and haul on the primary rode until you are half-

Fig. 9-8. Mooring buoy and pickup with staff (on deck)

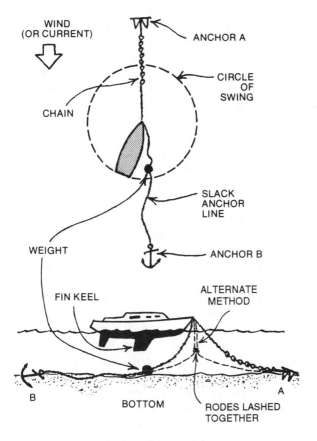

WIND
(OR CURRENT)

ANCHOR A

CIRCLE
OF
SWING

CHAIN

SLACK
ANCHOR
LINE

WEIGHT

ANCHOR B

FIN KEEL

ALTERNATE
METHOD

B

BOTTOM

RODES LASHED
TOGETHER

A

Fig. 9-9. Bahamian moor

way between anchors. If you have an all- chain rode, however, the chain may scar your topsides or bottom, so you
might want to back down after dropping the first anchor.

Usually, both rodes are led through bow chocks, and
the boat's circle of swing is little more than her length (see
illustration), but with a deep fin keel there is a possibility
of the keel fouling on the rode that leads astern. To alleviate this problem use a chain leader or a kellet to hold the
rode down. Another alternative is to attach one rode to the
other (normally with a rolling hitch) outboard of the bow
roller, and then pay out scope until the point of attachment is below the boat's keel. Anchoring from the bow
and stern to prevent swinging is not advisable except in
calm weather because the boat will not be able to hold her
bow into the seas.

Mediterranean Moor
In parts of Europe and sometimes elsewhere, boats use
the Mediterranean mooring system, whereby a bow anchor is dropped not far from a quay, and the boat is
backed into a narrow space between two moored vessels.
When the stern is close to the quay, stern lines from each
quarter are put ashore. This maneuver is often difficult
unless the wind is light, there is little current, and the
boat backs well. In unfavorable conditions, it could be
necessary to carry a stern line ashore in a dinghy after the
mother vessel has anchored. Then the stern can be pulled
or winched in to close proximity with the quay.

Another method of putting a stern line ashore is shown
in the accompanying illustration which shows a difficult
beam wind situation. By this method the boat goes into
the space bow first (step 1); a line is put ashore from the
bow (step 2); she backs out while paying out the line and
turns her stern into the wind when clear of the neighbor-

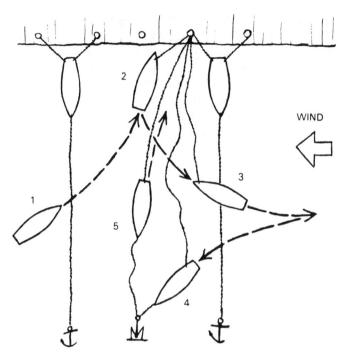

Fig. 9-10. Mediterranean moor, bow approach

ing vessel's anchor line (step 3); she then goes ahead and
her bow is turned away from the quay (step 4); the anchor
is dropped from the bow, and then the boat is hauled
back to the quay with the stern line while the anchor rode
is paid out slowly.

A simpler plan is to enter the slip or space between
moored vessels bow first after dropping an anchor from
the stern. Then moor with the bow, rather than the stern,
facing the quay. This method assures easier arrival and
departure while affording greater privacy due to the cock-

pit being away from the quay. A disadvantage is that it is more difficult to board and leave the boat by way of the bow; however, there are now special bow pulpits that have openings or gates to allow easier embarkment and disembarkment. Such an arrangement may make sense for a knockabout (boat without a bowsprit) having a long reverse transom or outboard rudder, as it will obviate the need for a long gangway at the stern.

10. Boat Care and Maintenance

From the bright lights of the beautiful yacht I returned to my scraper and paint brush.—Harry Pidgeon

The important part of boat maintenance is not what makes her look pretty but what keeps her seaworthy. No need to be overly concerned with spit and polish, but don't neglect the grease and paint that preserves and protects.

ROUTINE CARE

Many modern boats made of fiberglass, with a minimum of brightwork and brass, and with synthetic running rigging and sails, require relatively little maintenance compared with the fancy wooden yachts of earlier times. Nevertheless, every vessel must contend with the ravages of the sun, wind, salt, water saturation, and marine growth as well as gradual deterioration through aging. Here are some preventative maintenance and TLC (tender loving care) suggestions that should be part of the boater's regular routine:

— Tie off your halyards so that they cannot beat the mast in windy weather. This is especially true with wire halyards that can chafe and scar a mast whether it is made of wood or aluminum.

— Lines are forever coming unravelled on a boat, and they should be attended to with reasonable promptness. As stated in Chapter 2, a needle whipping with waxed thread is the most seamanlike method to deal with cows' tails, but I find that a quick repair that holds up for a surprisingly long time consists of: wrapping the line just below the unravelled end with electrical tape, cutting off the line just above the tape, and then melting the end of the line (when synthetic) with a flame.

— Constantly lubricate your gear to combat corrosion and malfunctioning. Use a light oil such as 3-in-one on such gear as spinnaker pole pins and screw fittings. Be sure your winches do not make an audible grinding noise or become gummy (spin them to see) because a sticking pawl or spring could cause a serious injury (see Chapter 2). Every year or so winches should be disassembled and cleaned, then lubricated with a product recommended or made by the winch manufacturer such as Lewmar winch grease or Barlube (don't use on pawl springs). Lanolin is often recommended as a lubricant for turnbuckles and clevis (non-threaded) rigging pins.

— Some deck gear, such as traveler slides, jib lead cars, pelican hooks, blocks, and sheaves should not be heavily greased, as this encourages a buildup of dirt and salt which hinders operation. Frequently flush these fittings with fresh water, and occasionally spray with a light lubricant and cleaner such as WD-40. Sticky fittings that are fouled with dirt or bird droppings can be freed with very hot water. Silicone spray lubricants are good for most sticking, binding, or squeaking surfaces such as sliding hatch covers.

— Every so often, spray a moisture-displacing cleaner/lubricant such as WD-40, CRC 6-66, or Gly Spray Lubricant on electrical terminals and connections.

— Periodically check the fluid level of your batteries. As noted in Chapter 7, maintain a level of between ¼ and ½ inch above the plates. When fluid is low add distilled water, but when none is available, use clean drinking water.

—Clean up bird droppings as soon as you can, because they can leave stubborn stains and even eat holes in cloth covers. To combat such "foul play," use a plastic owl and/or the yellow balloons with eyes used by gardeners called Terroreyes. Be sure there is a staff or antenna at the masthead to prevent birds from perching there.

—Try cleaning deck stains with a nonabrasive cleaner such as Boat-Zoap. Stubborn marks on a skid-proof deck might need to be attacked with Comet and a stiff tooth-brush.

—The commonly seen yellow-brown stain at or just above the waterline is easily removed with a cleaner containing oxalic acid. Y-10 is an effective product for fiberglass hulls. Liberal use of boat wax will help prevent the forma-tion of topside stains.

—A homemade cleaner for rust stains is a mixture of salt and lemon juice.

—Diesel oil spillage can be deodorized with white vinegar.

—Be watchful for peeling tape that protects sails (and fingers) from sharp cotter pins. Renew the tape periodical-ly. Sticky gum from old tape can be removed with Bestine Solvent.

—Whenever possible, cover anything that is particularly vulnerable to UV (ultraviolet) degradation. This includes some varnished surfaces, sails subject to exposure, and the compass card. A cloth that is highly resistant to sun damage, yet allows some ability to "breathe," is acrylic cloth such as Acrylan. If you have a cockpit dodger with a front that can be opened to allow a flow-through of air, consider leaving the dodger up to protect the companion-way varnish, winches, and any plastic fittings in the vicinity.

Fig. 10-1. Author's boat with helmsman's awning (note owl above horseshoe buoy to scare off birds)

Fig. 10-2. The author holding a scarecrow balloon (similar to terroreyes) used to protect the boat from bird droppings

Fig. 10-3. Front-opening dodger

—Check for broken stitching in sails and covers. Heed
the old expression, "a stitch in time saves nine." Surprisingly, dark stitches seem to be more resistant to UV damage than white stitches, and failure is more easily spotted.
—Check for broken strands in the wire rigging. Running
a rag over the wire will save your fingers. An occasional
snag can be broken off close to the wire, but a number of
snags in one area indicates fatigue and the wire should be
replaced.
—As noted in Chapter 1, look for deck leaks, especially on
a wooden boat, because they can cause rot. Find the
source of the leak on a rainy day or by using a hose, and
stop the leak as soon as possible with caulking, sealing,
or bedding compounds or by regasketing. Silicone is a
good bedding compound where adhesion is not important,
while polysulfide is a good general purpose sealant afford-

ing some adhesion. Polyurethanes are good where adhesion is the major concern.

—A particularly troublesome spot that is subject to leakage is the maststep. See that there are drain holes and a tight boot (cover to prevent leakage where the mast penetrates the deck). If you have internal halyards you might plug the mast just below the lowest halyard exit as shown in the illustration. Details of the procedure can be found in my book *Understanding Rigs and Rigging*.

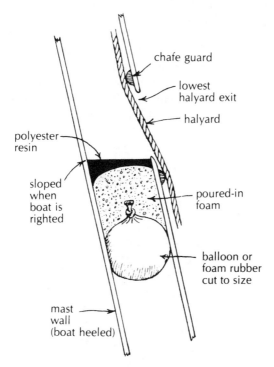

Fig. 10-4. Plugging the mast below the lowest halyard exit (note that boat is heeled before pouring resin) (From Understanding Rigs and Rigging *by Richard Henderson)*

— Use your nose, especially after the boat has been closed up for long periods, to detect dry rot and gasoline fumes. As stated earlier, gas fumes are highly explosive, and dry rot, which has a very musty odor, can spread rapidly.

— See that your boat is well ventilated when you leave her, as this helps prevent rot, mildew, and the buildup of fumes. Have plenty of Dorades (see Chapter 1) or other water trap ventilators and see that there are ample ventilation slats on the companionway drop boards. To obtain the maximum amount of air flow belowdecks, I use a large bow vent facing forward and hang a bucket under it in the forepeak as illustrated. All lockers should be open when the boat is left moored, and there should be ample ventilation holes, louvers, or slots in all doors.

— Wet sails that are stowed below should not be bagged until they are dry. You can bag dry parts of the sail, but see that wet parts are loosely spread out to dry. Wet sails

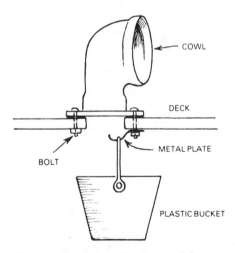

Fig. 10-5. Using a bucket under forward-facing vent

left bent on the boom and covered should be hoisted to dry at the first possible opportunity on a moderately calm day. See that your sail covers are loose fitting to assure some air circulation under the cover.

— Adjust your backstay tension. Set the stay taut for sailing but slack it off when leaving the boat for any length of time.

— Exercise your sea cocks, especially gate valves. Even if they are continually left open, close them occasionally so that they won't become frozen or difficult to operate due to corrosion. As mentioned in Chapter 3, when the boat is left for a period of time, keep closed all sea cocks except those for scuppers or an automatic bilge pump.

— Keep the bilge and sumps as dry as possible. Occasionally inspect the bilge limber holes and keep them open by prodding with a rod or piece of stiff wire. Do the same with any drain holes. Especially check the drain on any locker that holds LP (liquid petroleum) gas tanks.

— See that all air vents for tanks are protected and clear (clogged vents have actually caused tank damage).

WINTER LAYUP

As a general rule, wooden boats are best left afloat during the winter in areas where ice is not excessive. In her natural element, a boat is evenly supported so that the hull will not lose its shape and seams will not open up because of the wood drying out. On the other hand, most fiberglass boats are best stored on shore during the winter to guard against osmotic blistering. This results from water permeating the gel coat of a fiberglass boat and dissolving water-soluble materials in the laminate. When this occurs, an acid solution is formed which attempts to escape, thereby generating pressure and causing blisters.

The problem is alleviated by giving the boat periodic opportunities to dry out. Here are some decommissioning and layup suggestions:

—When the boat is dry stored (stored on shore), see that she is leveled (with the waterline parallel to the ground) so that scuppers will perform as intended.

—Be sure that a dry-stored boat is well supported. There should be ample supports distributing pressure over wide areas of the hull, and make sure that poppets (boat stands or jackstands) or cradles are sturdy and secure. The legs of boat stands should be chained together to prevent possible slippage.

—See that there is a drain in the low part of the bilge which is left open during dry storage.

—Boats that are wet stored (left afloat) in areas where ice is apt to form need a water agitator or bubble system to inhibit ice formation. Thin, sharp ice tends to do the most damage, especially in areas where there is current.

—Be sure your mooring lines are in good shape and are well protected from chafe. Cross your stern lines and use springs to inhibit boat movement. Allow for tides that are greater than normal summer tides, and use plenty of fenders. Check the lines on neighboring boats.

—The only seacocks left open on wet stored boats should be those servicing scuppers, and they should be protected from ice by inserting soft rubber hoses or tubes through the scuppers when their outlets are below the waterline. Lubricate seacocks and gate valves.

—Remove any gear such as sails, bedding, linen, etc., that is subject to mildew. If your boat is dry and well ventilated, this may not be necessary.

—Stored sails should be folded or preferably rolled when they are laminated, then bagged and stored in a dry, ro-

Fig. 10-6. A simple Jowi steel cradle supporting the author's miniature yacht, a Cape Dory Typhoon

dent-free place. Fold lines should run parallel to the foot. Jibs are best rolled (from head to foot).

—Water tanks need draining, and in cold regions anti-freeze should be put in sink drains and the water closet (WC). Winterize holding tanks according to manufacturer's instructions.

—Check the tightness of all hose clamps. This is especially important if your boat is wintering afloat.

—Spray your tools and electrical fittings with a light lubricant, such as WD-40.

—Whether dry- or wet-stored, boats are best protected with a proper winter cover. This should be supported by a frame, normally consisting of a wooden ridge pole (on the boat's centerline) held up with supports that go to the toe rail. Covers should be made of a material that is sun resistant and can "breathe" (such as Acrylic, Sunbrella, or Argonaut). Be sure there is ample air circulation under the cover by providing ventilation ports (holes protected with hoods) and perhaps leaving spaces between the rail and cover. If you don't want to cover the entire deck, at least have a cover large enough to protect the cockpit and companionway.

— A varnished wooden mast is usually removed to preserve its finish, but it should be handled and stored with great care. When stored off the floor it needs multiple supports to assure that it will not bend or warp. Aluminum masts can be left stepped, but external halyards should be removed, and most masts should be removed every few years for thorough inspection and servicing. It is good practice to slightly slack off the standing rigging. Mark the tuned position (rigging tension for optimal sailing) with tape on the turnbuckle's threads.

— Batteries should be taken off the boat and stored in a cool, dry place. They should be cleaned, and it is recommended that they be fully charged once a month.

— Engine layup includes: changing the engine and transmission oil, draining at low points the water jackets and piping (renew antifreeze in undrained freshwater cooling systems); and protecting the cylinder walls by coating them with a thin film of lubricating oil. The latter is done by squirting oil into the inlet manifold and cranking the engine a few times by hand to spread the oil. Plug air inlets and exhaust pipes. If, like me, you are not mechanically inclined, it is best to use a good yacht yard or professional mechanic for servicing the engine.

— There are two schools of thought concerning fuel tanks. One advocates emptying the tanks to prevent possible deterioration of the fuel, and the other advocates filling the tanks to avoid condensation. The latter is the easiest method, but draining a tank provides better assurance of clean, uncontaminated fuel in the spring. In any event, don't leave the tanks partially full, and plug the air vents (make a note of this to assure that the vents are unplugged at the time of commissioning the engine).

SPRING COMMISSIONING

Although many boats in tropical or semitropical waters are kept in commission all year, boats in colder climates are winterized in the manner just discussed and then dewinterized and commissioned every spring. Even those craft left in commission all year are normally refurbished in the spring. This is a happy time of year for the boater, but there is plenty of work to be done by a service yard and/or the owner. This work includes the following:

— Remove the winter cover. Check for broken stitching and chafed areas. If repairs are needed, have them made as soon as possible. See that reinforcements and anti-chafe patches are added where needed.

— Hose down and clean the decks and topsides. This is a good time to install state registration tags (if the boat is not documented). They are normally stuck on the topsides at the bow next to the registration number.

— Clean and smooth the boat's bottom, and then apply antifouling paint. Tin-based paints are now banned for all but aluminum yachts, but copper-based paints are still legal and reasonably effective in repelling barnacles and marine growth. For non-racers at least, especially those in warm sea water, it generally makes sense to choose a bottom paint containing a high percentage of cuprous oxide, as high as 60 to 75 percent.

— If your fiberglass boat has a few bottom blisters, pop them, dig out loose or soft material, wash with fresh water, and let the area dry thoroughly. Then sand well, remove dust, and apply an epoxy barrier coat such as VC-Watertite or InterProtect. Severe blistering may require removal of the gel coat, months of drying, and a generous epoxy coating of the entire underbody prior to painting with antifoulant.

— Clean and polish the propeller. If you paint the prop with antifoulant, a recommended procedure is first to apply a barrier coat of epoxy before applying the antifoulant to improve adhesion and protect against corrosion.

— Renew the sacrificial zinc collar on the prop shaft even though its absence may discourage barnacles on the prop. The discouragement of barnacles is not worth the risk of serious corrosion (see Chapter 1).

— Fiberglass topsides should be waxed, but if they are badly scratched or faded, consider painting them with one of the new, extremely durable polyurethane coatings such as Awlgrip. Imron and Sikkens are more easily repaired, but Awlgrip excels in durability. These coatings are best applied by a boatyard and they are expensive, but with proper care in docking, they can last for many years.

— Metal hulls need careful attention at commissioning time, as rust is a problem with steel, and aluminum boats in salt water are especially subject to galvanic corrosion. In painting a metal hull, it is important to follow carefully the directions of the paint manufacturer with regard to preparation, undercoatings, and application. It may well pay in the long run to use the so-called "high performance" paints such as two-part epoxies or polyurethanes for extra longevity. Steel hulls need painting on the inside as well as the outside. On any metal boat avoid using

Fig. 10-7. Sacrificial zincs on a prop shaft and strut (note rubber tube through scupper outlet to prevent damage from ice)

dissimilar metals and incompatible bottom paints (for example, copper or mercury paints on aluminum hulls); otherwise use a barrier between metals, such as multiple coatings of epoxy. Where the law allows, use tin-based antifoulants on aluminum hulls. Sacrificial zincs are especially important on metal hulls. They should be inspected frequently and perhaps renewed. Never paint them.

—Traditionally, woodwork above the deck was varnished, but many modern boaters with teak trim prefer to leave it raw or oiled to reduce maintenance. At commissioning time raw teak should be thoroughly cleaned with a chemical cleaner, rinsed with water, and then treated with a sealer (I've had success with Te-Ka cleaner and Semco sealer). Oiled teak is a compromise between varnish and raw teak. Some sailors are partial to Deks Olje (DO), which can provide either a matte finish using DO No.1 alone or a gloss finish more like varnish by overcoating DO No.1 with DO No. 2. This system requires frequent touching up and occasional recoating, but most agree that Deks Olje is easier to maintain than varnish.

— Preparation of the wood surface prior to painting and especially varnishing often requires liberal use of sandpaper. Begin sanding with fairly course grit paper and finish with fine grit. A full sheet of sandpaper should be folded as illustrated so that the rough sides do not make contact with each other. Fold it into quarters, then unfold and tear along one seam until reaching the center of the paper. Then fold each quarter over the other so that no gritty surface touches another. This makes the paper easier to use and longer lasting.

— The secret of maintaining varnish is to keep after it. Anytime there is a scratch or blemish, sand and touch up promptly. Once the spot becomes weathered it will turn dark and will have to be bleached. Be sure that bare wood, particularly teak, is properly sealed with a recommended sealer. Apply multiple varnish coats with the first coats well thinned and later coats progressively thicker. Sand lightly between coats and use a tack cloth to remove the dust. Many sailors prefer polyurethane varnish belowdecks but softer spar varnish above decks for easier maintenance.

— Vacuum the cabin, and clean the stove, especially the burners. Be sure the stove fuel lines are sound and tightly secured.

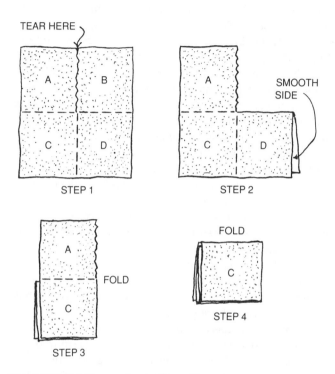

Fig. 10-8. Folding a sheet of sandpaper

— Inspect the steering system for play, binding, or wear, and lubricate if necessary. Check the cables for proper tension, security, and smoothness of operation. If the boat is out of water, examine the rudder heel fitting.

— Commissioning the engine includes the following steps: unplug air inlets and the exhaust pipe, clean and adjust distributor points, clean and set gap on spark plugs (renew if necessary), inspect wiring and tighten connections, check all hoses and belts, fill grease cups, grease and exercise control cables, inspect fuel lines and service filters, check lube oil in engine and transmission and change filter, flush the fresh water cooling system, reinstall batteries and clean terminals, adjust the stuffing box (where prop shaft penetrates hull) so that there is a very slow drip when the engine is running, check engine alignment, and see that ample water is flowing from exhaust.

— Lubricate the water closet with cooking oil or special toilet lubricants such as Sudbury Marine Toilet Conditioner or Sea-Lube. After closing seacock, remove intake hose and pour a bit of oil into it.

— Check all hose clamps everywhere, exercise and lube seacocks, and needless to say, insert the drain plug before launching.

— Reinstall any electronics that were removed during the winter. Clean contacts.

— Check all navigation and cabin lights. Test dry cell batteries and renew where necessary.

— Check for compass deviation as explained in Chapter 6.

— Carefully inspect the mast and, if it was removed, the mast step. Check the spreader fittings, tangs, and terminal fittings to see that there is no corrosion, deformation, or insecurity. Look especially for stress cracking (see Chapter 2). Examine fastenings, sheaves, lights, mast boot, and the spreader tips for security and integrity of antichafe gear. Wood spars are preferably varnished rather than painted, as the transparency of varnish allows inspection of the wood for rot.

— Tune the rig. See that the mast is vertical and straight, when viewed from the fore-and-aft direction, and raked aft slightly (about 1 foot of rake for every 35 feet of luff length is the general rule) to hang the mainsail properly and balance the helm. Standing rigging should be set up in accordance with the suggestions in Chapter 2. Wipe down the wire rigging with a rag to clean and also to check for snags.

Spring commissioning should provide a shipshape boat that is ready for sea. But bear in mind that seamanship (including maintenance) is an ongoing art that must be practiced throughout the entire boating season. Much of the pleasure derived from this practice is obtained by striving for the elusive goal of perfection.

Select Bibliography

Armstrong, Bob. *Getting Started in Powerboating.* Camden, Me.: International Marine Publishing Co., 1990.

Ashley, Clifford. *The Ashley Book of Knots.* New York: Doubleday, 1944.

Beebe, Robert P. *Voyaging Under Power.* New York: Seven Seas Press, 1975.

Bell, David Owen. *Dockmanship.* Centreville, Md.: Cornell Maritime Press, 1992.

Bowditch, Nathaniel. *American Practical Navigator* (Pub. No. 9). 2 vols. Washington, D.C.: U.S. Government Printing Office, 1984.

Brindze, Ruth, ed. *Experts' Book of Boating.* Englewood Cliffs, N.J.: Prentice-Hall, 1959.

Calder, Nigel. *Boatowner's Mechanical and Electrical Manual.* Camden, Me.: International Marine Publishing Co., 1990.

———. *Repairs at Sea.* Camden, Me.: International Marine Publishing Co., 1988.

Coles, K. Adlard. *Heavy Weather Sailing,* 3d rev. ed. New York: John DeGraff, 1981.

Colin, A.T. *Anchors and Mooring.* London: The Maritime Press, Ltd., 1963.

Cruising Club of America Technical Committee. *Desirable and Undesirable Characteristics of Offshore Yachts,* ed. John Rousmaniere. New York: W.W. Norton, 1987.

Dellenbaugh, David, ed. *The North U. Cruising Course.* Milford, Conn.: North Sails, 1990.

Fagan, Brian M. *Anchoring.* Camden, Me.: International Marine Publishing Co., 1986.

Graumont, Raoul. *Handbook of Knots.* Centreville, Md.: Cornell Maritime Press, 1990.

Henderson, Richard. *Sea Sense.*, 3d. ed. Camden, Me.: International Marine Publishing Co., 1991.

———. *Sail and Power*, 4th ed. Annapolis, Md.: Naval Institute Press, 1991.

———. *Sailing in Windy Weather.* Camden, Me.: International Marine Publishing Co., 1987.

———. *Understanding Rigs and Rigging,* rev. ed. Camden, Me.: International Marine Publishing Co., 1991.

Hinz, Earl R. *The Complete Book of Anchoring and Mooring,* 2d ed. Centreville, Md.: Cornell Maritime Press, 1994.

———. *Understanding Sea Anchors and Drogues.* Centreville, Md.: Cornell Maritime Press, 1987.

Hiscock, Eric. *Cruising Under Sail,* 3d ed. New York: Oxford University Press, 1981.

Jordan, Donald J. and Carol L. Hervey. "A Drogue Design to Prevent Breaking Wave Capsize." Groton, Conn.: U.S. Coast Guard R & D Center, 1988.

Jorgensen, Eric. *Sailboat Maintenance.* Los Angeles: Clymer Publications, 1975.

Kinney, Francis S. *Skene's Elements of Yacht Design.* New York: Dodd, Mead & Co., 1973.

Kotsch, William J. *Weather for the Mariner,* 3d rev. ed. Annapolis, Md.: Naval Institute Press, 1983.

——— and Richard Henderson. *Heavy Weather Guide,* 2d. ed. Annapolis, Md.: Naval Institute Press, 1984.

MacEwen, W.A. and A.H. Lewis. *Encyclopedia of Nautical Knowledge.* Centreville, Md.: Cornell Maritime Press, 1953.

MacGibbon, James, trans. *New Glenans Sailing Manual.* Boston: Sail Books, Inc., 1978.

Maloney, Elbert S. *Dutton's Navigation and Piloting*, 14th ed. Annapolis, Md.: Naval Institute Press, 1985.

―――. *Chapman's Piloting, Seamanship, and Small Boat Handling*, 60th ed. New York: Hearst Marine Books, 1991.

Melton, Luke. *Piloting with Electronics*. Camden, Me.: International Marine Publishing Co., 1987.

Meisel, Tony. *Nautical Emergencies*. New York: W.W. Norton & Co., 1984.

Noel, Jr., J.V. *Knight's Modern Seamanship*, 14th ed. New York: D. Van Nostrand, 1966.

Rousmaniere, John. *Annapolis Book of Seamanship*. New York: Simon and Schuster, 1989.

Schult, Joachim. *The Sailing Dictionary*. London: Adlard Coles, Ltd., 1981.

Taylor, Roger C. *Knowing the Ropes*, 2d ed. Camden, Me.: International Marine Publishing Co., 1993.

―――. *Elements of Seamanship*, 2d ed. Camden, Me.: International Marine Publishing Co., 1986.

U.S. Coast Guard. *Navigation Rules, International—Inland*. Washington, D.C.: Government Printing Office, 1983.

Waters, John M. *A Guide to Small Boat Emergencies*. Annapolis, Md.: Naval Institute Press, 1993.

Watts, Alan. *Instant Weather Forecasting*. New York: Dodd, Mead & Co., 1968.

Williams, Margaret. *The Boater's Weather Guide*. Centreville, Md.: Cornell Maritime Press, 1990.

Index

About the Author

Living on a bank of the Chesapeake Bay at Gibson Island, Maryland, Richard Henderson, known as "Jud" to his friends, is one of the nautical world's most prolific writers. His twenty books include such widely acclaimed titles as *Hand, Reef, and Steer*; *Sea Sense* (3d edition); *Single-handed Sailing* (2d edition); *Understanding Rigs and Rigging*; *Choice Yacht Designs*; *Philip L. Rhodes and His Yacht Designs*; *John G. Alden and His Yacht Designs* (with R.W. Carrick); *Heavy Weather Guide* (with W.J. Kotsch); *The Racing Cruiser* (2d edition); and *Sail and Power* (4th edition), the official textbook of the U.S. Naval Academy. Henderson's knowledge of the sea comes from more than sixty years of sailing, beginning at age six.

In a series of boats named *Kelpie*, Henderson has raced successfully (fifteen seasonal High Point awards) and taken numerous cruises, the longest being a family trans-atlantic crossing made with his wife and two children aboard a 37-foot sloop. In other boating-related activities he has done advisory work as a member of the American Boat and Yacht Council, been nautical advisor for Expeditions Limited, and served as a board member/writer for The Telltale Compass. Henderson's most recent boat is a Cape Dory Typhoon, the classic Alberg-designed miniature yacht. Boating aside, his principal hobbies are collecting jazz records and playing the piano.